"In this easy to understand a offers 47 excellent tips organ managing organizations in to world This book is a must read for anyone aspiring to be an effective executive in contemporary organizations."

Lawrence Korb - *Senior Fellow, Center for American Progress; former Assistant Secretary of Defense; and a retired navy captain.*

———

"Michael has brought nostalgic notions into sharp focus for today's leader. His analysis is thorough, the stories engaging and the gentle reminder that we can all improve our own Empathetic Leadership. This was profoundly demonstrated in Tip #25: Fierce Conversations, underscoring how kindness and honesty are vastly different than a cruel tweet or anonymous comment that we see on social media. Vintage is hip. Upcycling and reusing the old is good for our environment, our teams and even our hearts!"

Gwen Taylor - *Personal Development Trainer, Founder, GwenTaylor.com*

———

Empathetic Leadership is a great read for both the seasoned and new leader. It serves as a reminder that sometimes we make relationship building too hard and if we just remember what we learned in kindergarten and treat others as we would want to be treated, then we have a win/win. An uncomplicated guide to effective leadership.

Christine Kay – *Director of Citizen Services, Carroll County Government (Carroll County, Maryland)*

———

We've all heard the term he/she is a "born leader." Fortunately, for the rest of us, leadership can be a learned trait. Empathetic Leadership is a short, well written, easy-to-read, excellent text combining the tried-and-true maxims of leadership with every day practical experiences. It combines these lessons with easy to remember stories which drive the message home.

It can be read as a manual for anyone in a management or HR position or simply by people looking to have better relationships with their family, friends, coworkers and others. The book is a quick read, with readily digestible lessons that can be implemented by all of us. The time-honored life lessons, which form the core of the book, need to be repeated to become a habit forming. Those who read and **reread** Empathetic Leadership will not only learn to lead with empathy and enjoy their own work, home, and life experience more than those who don't, but they will also have the added benefit of empowering employees and companies to perform at top level.

Empathetic Leadership is the perfect text for any manager or simply any person who wants to lead a more fruitful life while pursuing whatever their and their company's dreams.

Robert J. DeSousa, esq. - *State Director, Office of U.S. Senator Pat Toomey (Pennsylvania); Past President, Federal Bar Association*

———

With leadership lessons from professional baseball, the NFL, and Charlie Brown, Michael's stories about how empathetic leadership makes a difference in organizations are relatable and relevant to today's business environment. I found myself reflecting on my own experiences, thinking about how situations, organizations and leaders I have encountered have demonstrated empathy, or could have used more of it.

Empathetic Leadership also reminds us that the old idea of "Do Unto Others" the core premise of empathy, is still very relevant. These 47 tips illustrate through Michael's expansive HR experience how empathy makes a difference to the bottom line.

MIT, Harvard Business Review and Adam Grant all agree that soft skills are going to differentiate workers and leaders the coming years. Empathy is core to these skills and Empathetic Leadership is a great collection of practical tips and advice that illustrate how we can exercise this skill in our everyday business lives, for the betterment of our organizations.

James Cambareri – *VP/Director of Strategic Business Solutions, Publicis Groupe – ReSources USA*

In a world that is brash to the extreme, a book about empathetic leadership is like good vitamins. Michael, a seasoned professional in human resources, gives clear, actionable items that help you look at the place of empathy in today's workplace. You will walk away with new ideas and new skills that can only lead to positivity and collaboration with colleagues.

Sylvia Lafair PhD, President of Creative Energy Options (CEOinc), author of Don't Bring It To Work, top 30 global leadership guru; and creator of award-winning Total Leadership Connections program.

Empathetic Leadership truly centered my beliefs in leadership. In this hurried world of "getting it done quickly," Michael's book brought me back to my roots and reminded me what really works. This book brings it full circle. A must read.

Adela Gonzelez – President and CEO, Future Force Personnel Services

Empathetic Leadership is the best kind of leadership. What hit home most to me after reading this book is that if we remember to focus on caring for and developing our people, we'll be successful. As a leader, I don't need to teach my team more about our products. Most important to me is listening to them and then understanding how to build the best team to take care of our clients. It's all about people and culture!

Michelle Mindell --VP/ Senior Client Executive, Oswald Companies

Frankly, too many leaders think that being empathetic may be interpreted as weakness. Empathetic Leadership attacks that dangerous perception and courageously outlines how leaders can be MORE effective, MORE successful and MORE respected by being empathetic. My favorite book to share with leaders has always been Jesus CEO; now I have another "new favorite" to recommend!

Barbara Daush – Senior Consultant, Carney, Sandoe; former President, St. Agnes Academy – St. Dominic School (Memphis, TN)

Empathetic Leadership

47 Practical Tips for Leading with Kindness, Courage, and Confidence in An Age of Disruption

Michael Brisciana

≡[T]≡

Trust Publishing

Published by Trust Publishing
Editing by Margarita Martinez
Cover design by Aleksandra Dabic

DEDICATION

To my family, for your unending support and encouragement, and for showing me every day what it means to lead with kindness and empathy by the example of your lives.

CONTENTS

Tip #1: Keep Interviewing Until You Have the Perfect Fit
Tip #2: Hire Out of Excitement, Not Desperation
Tip #3: Take a Flyer on Potential
Tip #4: Continuously Adjust Your Talent Needs
Tip #5: Unleash Hidden Potential
Tip #6: Prepare New Managers
Tip #7: Assess the Costs and Benefits of Rock Stars
        and Role Players
Tip #8: Remember That You're Recruiting (and Retaining)
        the Whole Family
Tip #9: Recognize Connectors and Linchpins

Tip #10: Build Confidence
Tip #11: Use Reviews to Build Relationships
Tip #12: Delegate to Build Trust and Engagement
Tip #13: Engage All and Root for Their Success
Tip #14: Repair Relationships Through Service
Tip #15: Remember Maslow When Solving Problems
Tip #16: Promotions Can Change Lives
Tip #17: Expect the Right Things of Employees
Tip #18: Step Back to Solve the Right Problem
Tip #19: Have the Courage to "Counsel Out"

ACKNOWLEDGMENTS

With special thanks and appreciation to:

My managers and mentors, for your guidance and for all that you've taught me about leading with passion, purpose, and understanding

My colleagues (including many described in these pages), for generously sharing the benefits of your experience, wisdom, and knowledge throughout the years, and for your camaraderie, kindness, and encouragement

The employees and teams I have had the pleasure of supporting during my career, for your thoughtfulness and caring during great times and difficult days alike, for having patience when things didn't go as planned, and for sharing with me your hopes and dreams and trusting me to help you fulfill them in some small way

PREFACE

Several years ago, I had the occasion to capture my thoughts and reflections on HR and leadership topics in blog form, posting one hundred articles or so over a three-year period. A reflective person by nature, I greatly enjoyed the experience. So much that I really missed it when I stopped writing—which occurred when I quickly realized that my new job at a fast-paced, start-up-like company required my full attention.

Having a little time to once again reflect during a career transition this past summer, I revisited those blogs. With added experience and perspective, a selection of the articles around the topic of leadership stood out most to me. Seizing the chance to reshape my original thoughts, my new reflections coalesced strongly around the core idea of leading with empathy. A quick Google search revealed few, if any, books published directly on this topic—and with that, the "light bulb" went on, and this project was born!

As the project shaped up, I ended up revising, reforming, and inevitably, fully rewriting each of the articles. In doing so, I happily rediscovered the joy of writing and, in the process, decided to redirect my musings to a broader audience of leaders of all types of organizations (large, small, for-profit, nonprofit, etc.), rather than limiting my scope to my original blog's primary target of HR professionals. It has been a joyful, challenging, and enriching journey for me these past months. I hope that you find the resulting observations presented here useful as food-for-thought in your own leadership adventure.

Before we dive in to our exploration of leading with empathy, I want to share a few thoughts on how I've approached writing this book, as context.

Anecdotes Rather Than Formal Research

There are many truly brilliant leadership experts, researchers, and social scientists that can conduct and report on research into management techniques and the latest data-based understanding of leadership far better, deeper, and with more context than I possibly can (see Malcolm Gladwell, Simon Sinek, Travis Bradberry, Lolly Daskal, etc.). While that research influences the ideas expressed in this book, you will see little direct reference to studies, statistics, and the like here, which is purposeful. This isn't intended to dismiss such studies. They are vital, compelling, and crucial to our modern understanding of leadership.

In writing this book, though, I felt that I could best contribute my small part to the discussion by reflecting upon behaviors that I have personally observed in a variety of settings and which I believe are typical of many of the experiences of HR, business, government, and nonprofit leaders everywhere. I hope that you may find this approach relevant and beneficial to your own leadership journey.

Discretion and Privacy

Flowing from the book's reliance on personal anecdotes, there is a sensitive matter that I'd like to address upfront regarding discretion and privacy—notions that I care deeply about as an individual and as an HR person. Knowing that everyone's impressions of events, along with what they consider to be positive, negative, and neutral, can differ (sometimes widely), I've wrestled with the most accurate, appropriate, and discreet way to share some of the stories in this book.

Following the axiom that "we can learn from the good and the bad," I believe it is appropriate to include examples of shortfalls, stumbles, errors, and miscues in a book based on human behavior. As many of these negative examples describe my *own* errors in judgment, lack of self-awareness, and ill-conceived ideas and actions, discussing these was easy—and I hope that an apologetic spirit of *"mea culpa, mea maxima culpa"* comes through clearly on my part in those descriptions.

Commenting negatively on the behavior and actions of *others,* however, was more difficult for me to reconcile, as:

1. These were all talented, dedicated people who were trying to do their best for their organizations and their teams
2. As human beings, we all frequently come up short of the mark—so, who am I to judge the actions or errors of others?

That being said, as a book on leadership techniques wouldn't be worth very much without illustrating both "do's" *and* "don'ts," this is how I decided to approach things:

- **Discretion** – I have changed all names, positions, functions, and organizations and modified the business settings and circumstances in the vignettes described, to protect the privacy of all concerned
- **Goodwill** – I ask for the kind indulgence and understanding of any readers who I have worked or interacted with in the past who may suspect that they "see" themselves or others they know in these pages. Please trust that any critiques are offered solely for the illustration of the ideas expressed, so that we all may learn and grow in our leadership abilities. Thank you for your understanding that all are offered in a spirit of goodwill, respect, and discretion.

Recent References to Empathy

Despite the lack of published books directly on this topic, it has been exciting to see the increasing mention of ideas around "leading with empathy" in other formats (articles, videos, social media mentions, etc.) from business leaders, management experts, and academic researchers in recent years. As of this writing, Googling "leading with empathy" returns 51,400,000 results! A brief sampling:

- *How to Lead with Empathy: A new breed of CEOs is defined less by "command and control" and more by "inspire and empower." – Fast Company, 9/18/17*
- "Of all the leadership soft skills, empathy is arguably the most critical … leading to higher workforce productivity, and better business results." – Tacy Byham, CEO – DDI, leading global training firm, as quoted in the video "Why Empathy Really Matters," on the DDI website (www.ddiworld.com)
- *Why the Empathetic Leader is the Best Leader* – from www.lollydaskal.com – Lolly Daskal, global leadership expert, executive coach, author, and speaker
- *Leading with Empathy* – graduate course led by Dr. Xuan Zhao at the University of Chicago, Booth School of Business
- *The Secret to Leading Organizational Change is Empathy* – Patti Sanchez, HBR.org Daily, 12/20/18

Looking Forward

I am eager to follow ever-increasing interest on this topic in the media, in academia, and the economy and culture in general in the coming months and years. I hope that this book adds to the breadth and depth of the ongoing discussion. I wish you great joy in the process of discovery, and I hope that you enjoy and benefit from the thoughts and examples offered in the following pages.

Michael Brisciana
Port Washington, NY, USA
December 2018

INTRODUCTION

Empathy
The ability to step into the shoes of another person, aiming to understand
their feelings and perspectives, and using that understanding
to guide our actions.
Roman Krznaric, Six Habits of Highly Empathetic People

In a hyper-changing world, organizations are increasingly seeking "leading edge" solutions to their issues. As the economy and our working lives become more and more complex and faster-paced, it seems logical for an executive to say, "Get me the latest thinking on this problem." And yet, I wonder ... is it really?

Do we want the latest solution—or the solution that's going to *work best*, even if it is "tried and true" (even mundane and boring)? Do we want to be leading edge for the purposes of image and cachet, and is the latest necessarily the greatest? Particularly when it comes to managing people, is there really anything new under the sun?

What's Old Is New: Value in Vintage
As you'll soon discover, there is little in this book that is necessarily new or innovative. It argues for the notion that timeless truths about human motivation and behavior have the greatest impact on leading and motivating others for the best and most lasting effect. In this way, it shares much in spirit with the ethos expressed in Robert Fulghum's classic tome, *All I Really Need to Know I Learned in Kindergarten:*

*Most of what I really need to know about how to live and what to do
and how to be I learned in kindergarten. Wisdom was not at the top of
the graduate school mountain, but there in the sandpile at Sunday school.*

I share Mr. Fulghum's belief that it is not necessary for something to
be new or shiny to be useful or relevant in our increasingly fast-paced
global business environment. Rather, it just has to speak to a deep-
rooted understanding of human nature and human behavior,
providing guidance for being a good manager, a good leader, a good
human being, and a contributor to the welfare of others.

I find that this holds true even (or especially) in our current age of
business disruption, where multibillion-dollar valuation "unicorn"
companies crop up seemingly overnight, creating technologies and
industries that didn't exist only a few years (or months) before.
Especially in these cases, a tried and true understanding of human
behavior may serve as a stabilizing force amidst the ever-present
winds of change and innovation.

History moves on and the world evolves, but at its core, human
nature—and what's productive, and not, in organizations— remains
the same. Ironically, that may make these old truths (I prefer to say
"timeless") hip and trendy again, given the recent nostalgia for
anything "vintage" or "retro." What's old is new, indeed.

Core Beliefs

In the end, it's not important whether something is old or new—just
that it works. I believe that both history and an observation of
modern behavior shows that people (i.e., employees, peers,
colleagues, subordinates, supervisors, and executives) respond better
to:

- Understanding over dismissiveness
- Humility over arrogance
- Welcoming in over shutting out

- Encouragement over rejection
- Support over derision
- Outreach over aloofness
- Sincerity over pretense
- Building up over tearing down

In an age in which we have come to recognize how vital inclusiveness is to our collective success, all the above qualities and actions speak directly to inclusion, authenticity, and empathy. If people sense that their leaders are willing to "walk a mile in their shoes" before judging or dismissing them, they repay that empathy and trust ten-fold with increased loyalty, dedication, and performance. I believe that it's as simple and as powerful as that.

In this way, leading with empathy is not only good for employees, it is also good for managers and organizations (and investors), too. As leaders, we just need to slow down, remember that this is so, and retrain ourselves to act this way, instead of operating with knee-jerk reactiveness to the supposed urgencies of the day. With resilience and steadfastness of purpose, we will get there—it just takes time, and practice, and commitment.

Special Note: Our discussion of empathy doesn't mean that managers can't challenge or hold their employees accountable to high standards. Indeed, all are necessary parts of being a good and effective manager. They just all need to be done considering the impact on employees and maintaining dignity and support for all concerned.

Leading with Empathy

This book makes the case that leading with empathy is among the most authentic, impactful, and effective types of leadership. What, then, is leading with empathy? In brief, empathetic leadership is all about:

- Seeking out, hearing, and understanding how employees (and candidates) see, feel, think about, and experience the organization, their work, and their managers and peers
- Factoring this information into managing individuals, teams, and the organization as a whole—fairly, supportively, respectfully, and engagingly
- Achieving maximum performance and results by balancing the needs of the employee and of the organization—and seeking the mutual benefit for both.

It is about understanding the needs and perspectives of others and using this understanding to guide our actions as leaders. Getting it down to a simple list of "do's and don'ts," Mr. Fulghum put it so well:

These are the things I learned:

> *Share everything.*
> *Play fair.*
> *Don't hit people.*
> *Put things back where you found them.*
> *Clean up your own mess.*
> *Don't take things that aren't yours.*
> *Say you're sorry when you hurt somebody.*
> *Wash your hands before you eat.*
> *Flush.*
> *Warm cookies and cold milk are good for you.*
> *Live a balanced life—learn some and think some and draw and paint and sing and dance and play and work every day some.*
> *Take a nap every afternoon.*
> *When you go out into the world, watch out for traffic, hold hands, and stick together.*
> *Be aware of wonder.*

If you replace the phrase "how to *live*" in the first quotation with "how to *lead*," you've summed up the essence of this book.

Historical and Contemporary Perspectives

More than forty years ago now, my dad wrote his master's thesis on "The Human Relations Approach to Management," arguing for the notion that treating people well is both the most ethical and most productive approach to managing. Going back further into the past century, in the 1920s and 1930s, managers learned about the Hawthorne Effect (where merely paying attention to employees increased performance) and later in the 1950s and 1960s, they contemplated "Theory X" and "Theory Y"(wrestling with the question of whether employees were internally motivated, or not, influencing whether leaders managed through discipline, rewards, or encouragement).

Since that time, we have seen any number of management theories come down the pike, from 1980's ideas around "Management by Walking Around" (Peters and Waterman), to 1990's thinking on empowerment and quality circles and musings on "followership." Bringing us up the present day, the 2000s and 2010s have brought us new thoughts on engagement and servant leadership.

Each of these approaches has truth and value—and all have been "leading edge" for a moment in time. In one way or another, all these historical leadership theories come back to a few central ideas:

- Listen for understanding; hear what is being said (or not said) out loud and in the margins
- Understand employees' wants and needs—take them seriously and care about them

- Treat people according to the maxim of "do unto others" (more about that, below)
- Remember that the people doing the job usually have the best ideas about how to do the job best
- Give people the resources they need to do the job ... then get out of the way and let them do it
- Help people see the "big picture" so that they know how their work helps the company and its customers
- Have the courage to make the tough calls, for the good of all—knowing that people want, need, respect, and expect a confident leader with steady, inspiring vision who will help move them forward.

Stepping back from the mad pace of modern business, we pause and reflect, remembering that the essence of leadership is improving performance. While business has evolved rapidly, human nature hasn't, and our wants and needs remain largely the same as in decades and centuries past—i.e., we all want recognition, appreciation, support, encouragement, growth, and development. Seen from that viewpoint, we suggest that the "old" human relations approach to management that we began with above—i.e., leading with empathy, kindness, and confidence—serves the needs of modern leaders (and followers) just as effectively as in years past.

Updating "Do Unto Others" from Gold to Platinum Today

To bring the historical maxim of "do unto others" into the present day, as well as to align it most directly with true empathy, we need to update it from the "Golden Rule" to the "Platinum Rule," as coined by author and entrepreneur, Dave Kerpen, in his 2016 book, *The Art of People:*

> *We all grow up learning about the simplicity and power of the Golden Rule: Do unto others as you would want done to you. It's a splendid concept except for one thing: Everyone is different, and the truth is that*

in many cases what you'd want done to you is different from what your partner, employee, customer, investor, wife, or child would want done to him or her.

With that in mind, I came up with the Platinum Rule: Do unto others as they would want done to them.

The Platinum Rule is decidedly more difficult than the Golden Rule. It's easy to know what you want, but it's much harder to put yourself in another person's shoes, walk around in them, and understand that person's perspective. But although it's harder to do that, it's much more powerful in business and in life.

© 2016 by Dave Kerpen – The Art of People: 11 Simple People Skills That Will Get You Everything You Want

The platinum rule is the essence of modern empathy—seeking to understand the situation from the other person's perspective and guiding our actions accordingly.

The Organization of This Book

The rubber meets the road, of course, when maxims turn into actions, habits, and practices. To that end, I have derived forty-seven practical tips for leading with empathy from my experience in observing, advising, and supporting leaders during my career. These are organized under six chapter headings, roughly corresponding to six major activities that managers undertake:

1. Building your team (hiring)
2. Managing your team (day-to-day leadership)
3. Developing your culture (based on company mission and values)
4. Leading by example (personal leadership)
5. Coaching and mentoring (developing teams and individuals)
6. Managing your career (charting a path forward)

Each of the tips is comprised of an example or two; a brief evaluation of the plusses and minuses of the situation and what we can learn from it; and finally, "An Empathetic Approach"—a reflection on how we can practice leading with empathy in situations like this in our daily working lives.

With that being said ... let's begin our empathetic leadership journey!

CHAPTER 1
BUILDING A TEAM

As an empathetic leader begins to build their team, they will naturally consider the skills and abilities that are needed to carry out the necessary functions of the team. They can't stop here, however. They need to reflect deeply on the culture that they're wishing to instill and discern what individual characteristics are needed to contribute to that culture. Only then will they recruit and hire accordingly.

The tips and anecdotes shared in this chapter include:

- Even if you get tired, keep recruiting until you find the person who is a perfect fit for your needs
- Never extend a job offer unless you're truly excited at the prospect of having that person on the team
- Sometimes it pays to take a risk on a diamond in the rough
- You'll need to adapt your strategy for finding and developing talent as the organization's needs grow and evolve
- The talent you're seeking may already be hiding in plain sight
- It's important to prepare new managers for what they're signing up for in their new roles
- Calculating the costs and benefits of star performers isn't as simple as it may appear
- Consider the whole person (and the whole family) to create the best candidate and employee experience

- Identify and seek out those who bring (and hold) your team together

TIP #1:
KEEP INTERVIEWING UNTIL YOU HAVE THE PERFECT FIT

"There are many things in life that will catch your eye, but only a few will catch your heart. Pursue these."
Michael Nolan, author

"Pleasure in the job puts perfection in the work."
Aristotle, philosopher

"Far and away the best prize that life offers is the chance to work hard at work worth doing."
Theodore Roosevelt, 26th President of the United States

"The two most important days in your life are the day you were born and the day you find out why."
Mark Twain, author

Did you ever meet someone who was doing *exactly what they were meant to do*? I once heard a priest relate a story from the pulpit about how he knew he wanted to be a priest from the age of six. Most of us don't know from quite such a young age what we want to be when we grow up. When we finally find our one true vocation, though, it makes all the difference in the world.

Empathetic leaders are always seeking to add people of passion and character to their teams—the type of people who wake up every day and want to rush into work to get started on doing what they love to do—because they know the effect such individuals have on customers, peers, and an organization as a whole. And they don't stop until they find them (even if the process is wearying and they're otherwise tempted to give up and settle for "good enough").

"I Love This Job"

A scene I'll never forget: Cold, dark February morning. Sophomore year in an all-boys, Catholic high school. A modular, trailer-like classroom. Western Civ, second period. Thirty fifteen-year-olds fidgeting, bored, and bundled up against the cold. The teacher walked into the room and slammed his grade book on the desk.

He had our attention!

We all sat up, expecting angry words about bad grades on an exam, or poorly-written papers, or something like that.

Instead, he loudly, boldly, exclaimed: ***"I love this job!"***

A Tale of the "Right Fit"

Mr. Mark Hainey. Twenty-four-years old. Skinny. Passionate. Utterly sincere. Being paid probably a dollar above the minimum required by law. And he had just declared to a roomful of adolescent boys that *he loved his job*. To say that we had never seen anyone do that before would be an understatement.

For the next few minutes, he explained whatever it was that had him so excited. I forget the exact situation that stirred his passion that morning, but his point was essentially this: *It's the mission, not the money.* He knew he could be earning more money teaching elsewhere or working in a different occupation.

He was single and still living with his parents, so he could afford to choose mission over money. But the point is, he felt so aligned with the mission of his employer, and so aligned with the school's culture and values, that he just had to tell someone about it.

Now, all in all, the school was a very positive, mission-driven place. (We were told that we were "the school with a difference," and while that was never quite explained in any detail, we all came to see and feel its truth through people such as Mr. Hainey). Yet it remained a pretty startling pronouncement—and one that has stuck with me almost four decades later.

Lessons

Mr. Hainey was exactly right, of course. Seeing things from his perspective:

- He had a job that he was very good at. (This was in the days before the internet, social media, and rating your teachers online. If any of those had existed, he certainly would have been rated highly by his young charges).
- He cared deeply about his subject (his "job duties") and his students (his "customers") and he wanted us to be just as excited by the material as he was.
- He believed in the mission of the school, and he clearly saw his role as contributing to the success and sustenance of the organization.
- And he had enough variety in his job (refereeing Intramurals, leading Government Club trips, etc.) that it sustained him through the inevitable dry spots in any role.

Mr. Hainey was the perfect fit for his job—and it for him. Lesson: When you find a candidate like this … *hire them immediately!*

Counterpoint

As hiring managers, we all want to hire—and retain—candidates like Mr. Hainey. I find, though, that sometimes managers weary of the process before discovering the right-fit candidate. The extreme example of this is the hiring manager who told me to hire the very first candidate we interviewed. I asked if she wanted to interview more of the small pool of candidates I had developed. She said it wouldn't be necessary.

I said, "Wow—this candidate must have really blown you away. She must be amazing!"

The manager replied, "She's okay. Nothing extraordinary."

Confused, I asked why she wanted to hire her without seeing others as a point of comparison.

"It's just not worth the bother," she explained. "It doesn't matter. She'll be good enough. We don't need anything more."

I went home dejected and deflated that day, for sure. Not worth the bother? It doesn't matter? You couldn't get further from the hiring goals of an empathetic leader, of course—someone who keeps going until they find their perfect fit.

AN EMPATHETIC APPROACH

Empathetic leaders strive to put the most highly-qualified, "best-fit" candidates in place in every position in their organizations. With the hundreds (and sometimes even thousands) of résumés flooding across our desks, this is often a daunting task. I have seen even the best managers get tired and frustrated so that they want to short-circuit the hiring process with a merely good-enough candidate. It is difficult not to lose heart. To give up. To say, "It doesn't matter."

It does matter, though. It matters to the organization – and to the candidate, too. Imagine the difference it makes walking into a job for the first time knowing that you were hired because your boss saw you as a "perfect fit" with the role – rather than as merely "a body" filling a slot.

Given the vagaries of human behavior, emotion, and motivation, it is often just short of impossible to look into someone's mind (much less their heart) and know for certain whether they'll perform well in a job, much less whether they will thrive. We all know this, of course—but we have to keep heart. For, when we get it right, it can affect the lives of the people involved (employees, coworkers, managers, customers) in a deep and meaningful way … even forty years later.

TIP #2:
HIRE OUT OF EXCITEMENT, NOT DESPERATION

"Desperate times call for desperate measures."
Benjamin Franklin

"I am convinced that nothing we do is more important than hiring and developing people. At the end of the day, you bet on people, not on strategies."
Lawrence Bossidy, CEO, Allied Signal

"Do not hire a man who does your work for money, but him who does it for the love of it."
Henry David Thoreau, American poet

They say that "to err is human." Indeed. Even the most experienced manager can make rookie hiring mistakes when desperate or tired or just wanting the process to be completed so they can get back to running the business. However, rarely does hiring out of desperation end well for anyone involved. Empathetic leaders remind themselves that it's about finding the right person, not about settling—and that hiring someone they're not excited about isn't fair to the candidate or the company.

Here are several tips for "protecting you from yourself" when recruiting becomes desperate.

Hiring Mistake #1: Hiring Out of Desperation
Mistakes that I've commonly seen born out of desperation include:

- **Overcompensating (aka, throwing out the baby with the bathwater)** – We were hiring for a supervisory position where the prior incumbent was very knowledgeable but had a contentious relationship with customers, wasn't able to streamline processes, and generally brought a "sky is falling" cloud to the workplace every day.

  In hiring a replacement, we were right to focus on candidates with strong customer service and analytical skills. However, we were wrong to focus on these aspects to the exclusion of the core skill needed in the job—subject matter competence. Unfortunately, this is a common error: trying to hire the *opposite* of the prior person and forgetting about all the good skills they brought to the job. Predictably, the new hire didn't last long.

- **Seeing what you want to see** – When your assessment of the candidate's answers is more hopeful than it is realistic, this is an indication that you're "reaching." This is what happened when we were hiring for an HR professional to conduct detailed due diligence and policy analysis for potential acquisitions—a position requiring excellent written communications skills.

  The candidate we hired was bright, hard-working, willing to do whatever was necessary to help the team, demonstrated passion for the field, and had a charismatic and engaging personality. Unfortunately, we overlooked the fact that English was a second language for the candidate and native-level proficiency in written communication was significantly lacking.

  Earlier, as a college student, I once hired a cook for our fraternity house who had no cooking skills at all. Desperate for candidates, and seeing how eager she was for the position, we offered her the job even with huge red flags. For instance, during the interview process, she failed to provide the requested sample menu because she "couldn't think of any meals." Unsurprisingly, her tenure in our kitchen—despite a great attitude—was short.

- **Overlooking poor references** –Relating back to the examples above, when I checked the references for the candidate for the HR position, it turned out that what they represented as an HR position was really a customer service and delivery position. Similarly, the references for the fraternity cook indicated that previously she was a pantry helper, not a cook. With this knowledge, these individual's struggles in the positions they were hired for became much easier to   understand.

- **Limited Candidate Pools** -The common theme for each of the above vignettes is that we had been recruiting for each position for several months, with very little to show for it. When we came across a candidate who was (finally) in the ballpark in terms of experience, we were thrilled—and we pushed them through the process. When you have only one candidate, it's very easy to delude yourself into ignoring obvious deficiencies.

In each case, we hired the candidate. They tried hard. They fit in well with coworkers. And … they didn't come close to working out. We soon came to a mutual understanding that this wasn't the position for them, and they departed.

Hiring Mistake #2: Making Half-hearted Offers
In the scenarios above, we were naively optimistic about the hires. The opposite situation is also problematic. One time, we were

struggling with a senior-level hire, who would be reporting directly to the CEO. After not coming to terms with our first-choice candidate, I convinced the CEO to reconsider the number-two candidate.

This was a mistake, as the CEO never developed a rapport with the candidate during either round of the process. Nevertheless, we were fatigued by the extended recruiting process and went ahead with the offer. The "truth will out," as they say—the CEO couldn't muster more than lukewarm enthusiasm in making the offer. The candidate correctly read this lack of excitement and turned us down without even making a counteroffer.

AN EMPATHETIC APPROACH

On the surface, it looked like we were doing a good thing by offering opportunities to eager candidates with good attitudes. In reality, though, we weren't doing anyone any favors. Out of desperation and recruiting fatigue, we overlooked important skills gaps that made it impossible for the candidates to succeed in these positions. While no permanent harm was done, it was certainly disruptive and disappointing, to say the least, for all concerned.

An empathetic leader will take a full view of the hiring situation and will have the foresight and compassion not to offer jobs to those with whom they have no rapport or excitement or who don't have a reasonable chance at succeeding.

In all of these cases, we ultimately picked ourselves up, dusted ourselves off, reengaged in the search process, and ultimately hired candidates who were much better fits with the needs of the organization. Patience and perseverance pay off!

TIP #3:
TAKE A FLYER ON POTENTIAL

"The will to win, the desire to succeed, the urge to reach your full potential ... these are the keys that will unlock the door to personal excellence."
Confucius, philosopher

"I'm a firm believer that most people who do great things are doing them for the first time. I'd rather have someone all fired up to do something for the first time than someone who's done it before and isn't that excited to do it again. You rarely go wrong giving someone who is high potential the shot."
Marc Andreessen, venture capitalist

During my career, I've spent a lot of time training managers to identify the job's key skills, experience, and characteristics, and then design the interview process to systematically address these issues. It's all very good advice—except when it's not. When staffing flexibility allows you to hire for a role based on potential, it's critical to include intangible qualities of passion, perseverance, commitment, and dedication high on the list of required skills for the role. In these cases, it is often the right time to take a chance on someone's heart rather than their strict work history. This story is about one of those times.

Standing Out
During the course of a two-day management training session that I was delivering, a young professional -- Darren, an African American man in his early thirties -- stood out as a person of high potential. As I was chatting with his manager after the training wrapped up, I commented that "He's someone I would hire on gut reaction."

"It's funny you should say that," the manager replied. "That's exactly what I did." Then he went on to tell me Darren's story.

Early Ambition

Darren grew up as one of six children in an underprivileged family. Despite difficult circumstances, he always had a feeling that life had something more in store for him. Acting on this belief, when he was in high school, he wrote letters to fifty elite private schools, saying, "While I'm not one of your traditional candidates, I have the drive to succeed at your school—and I promise you that no one will outwork me, ever. If you give me a chance, I'll make you proud." Forty-nine schools ignored his letter; one offered him a scholarship.

Moving Forward in Life

After excelling in private school, Darren went on to a fine college career, playing Division II basketball and maintaining a 3.2 GPA. After graduating, though, he found that work was hard to find in an economy in recession. One day, he met an IT manager at a job fair. They established a quick rapport, so much so that, just on gut instinct, the manager hired Darren as a junior member of the IT team.

Three years later, when several department members quit unexpectedly and management scrambled to recover, Darren stepped forward to throw his hat into the ring. Reprising his pitch from high school, he said, "You know how much I care about this organization. I promise no one will outwork me in trying to get the job done."

He was granted the position and the rest, as they say, is history. Darren is now considered one of the up-and-coming leaders in his organization. In addition to his IT duties, he spends considerable time serving as a role model, advisor, and confidant to minority males among the organization's clients.

Diamonds in the Rough – Worth the Risk?

We know that every position on your team is valuable. You interview intently, trying to find the best fit among candidates, leaving nothing to chance. Why, then, would anyone ever suggest hiring "off the cuff"?

Not every organization can afford "we-know-it-will-take-time-for-them-to-grow-into-the-job" positions, of course. But where you can afford a calculated risk or two, a "from the gut" hire sometimes is a very prudent risk—as long as you do so knowing exactly *why* you're hiring the individual.

In Darren's case, what he lacked in formal IT training and experience, he more than made up for in other performance characteristics like resilience, natural leadership skills, etc., that were critical to success in that organization. On this basis, he wasn't nearly as much of a risky hire as he may have appeared on the surface. At the same time, the manager was very clear with Darren as to what skills he had, what he lacked, and what he had to develop.

From Darren's perspective, if it didn't work out, there would be no hard feelings; he knew what he had to do to grow into the position. All he asked was for someone to believe in him, and to give him the opportunity to succeed.

Point of Contrast

This may sound like a contradiction of the prior lesson (Tip #2), where we warned against overreaching and hiring on hope rather than skills. The difference in the case of hiring for potential is that you are making the hire in the *full knowledge* that they don't currently have the skills required, but believe they have the natural attributes that will allow them to *acquire* the necessary skills. Your eyes are wide open. You know that you're hiring on potential, and you're doing so purposefully.

27

AN EMPATHETIC APPROACH

Taking prudent chances like this can change lives. It certainly did so for Darren, and for everyone to whom he spreads the message of maximizing your potential through hard work. The manager saw that Darren was up for the opportunity and he also saw the positive message that putting Darren in a position to grow and succeed would mean to the culture of the organization. A "win-win," for sure.

TIP #4:
CONTINUOUSLY ADJUST YOUR TALENT NEEDS

"Develop talent for tomorrow, rather than just hire for yesterday."
Pearl Zhu, IT Innovation: Reinvent It for the Digital Age

"Talent management deserves as much focus as financial capital management in corporations."
Jack Welch, CEO, General Electric

"Talented people are vital to our continued success, and we continuously invest in our associates, giving them the tools and training to succeed."
Indra Nooyi, CEO, PepsiCo

The worldwide success of the *Harry Potter* book series and movie franchise has been a once-in-a-generation phenomenon. The decade-long endeavor to bring each of the books to life on the silver screen offers several lessons in casting (hiring) and talent management. This relates directly to empathetic leaders, who are continually scanning their environments to ensure that their hiring, development, and support processes are meeting the needs of their candidates and employees, as well as the evolving needs of the organization.

Using the *Harry Potter* films as a backdrop, several lessons come into focus:

- *Hire for talent – then provide them the support they need*
  It is a unique challenge to hire young actors (employees) on whose shoulders rest the fortunes of a worldwide, billion-

dollar franchise. While few of us will have recruiting
challenges of this exact type, all leaders face the daily
challenge of picking appropriate talent—and then providing
support that enables employees to succeed as the
organization's needs evolve and develop.

For the movies, this meant putting in place the right support
structures of directors, coaches, tutors, etc., around the young
actors to provide protection and guidance. In business,
leaders need to provide employees with appropriate resources
to support them (such as Employee Assistance Programs)
and address their growth needs (such as coaching and
professional development opportunities).

- *Communicate the vision and get others to buy in*
  The HP movies attracted a veritable "who's who" of
  esteemed U.K. actors (e.g., Maggie Smith, Kenneth Branagh,
  Emma Thompson, etc.). Even those in the smallest bit parts
  were aligned with the tone and style of the material. They
  bought into the author and producers' vision for creating a
  magical world on-screen and their performances, imbued
  with this spirit, brought a rich flavor to even the tiniest nooks
  and crannies of the films.

In much the same way, employees at all levels extend and
support the organization's vision in their daily work—or
not—in ways that are ultimately felt and seen by the
customers. If the organization's stars are not bought into the
"premise" (i.e., the mission) and are just going through the
motions, the company will lose its forward momentum in
fairly short order. Conversely, though, if everyone in the
organization is operating out of the same playbook, great
things are possible every day.

- *As organizational needs evolve, so do talent needs. Adapt accordingly.*

  J.K. Rowling's material evolved dramatically over the course of the seven-book series, from innocent childhood fantasy to darker themes of struggle, sacrifice, and the ultimate battle between good and evil. The producers wisely hired directors for each film whose talents were aligned with the relative gravity of the material.

So, too, do products and projects evolve in an organization, and matching talent appropriately at each stage of a product/project's life is critical to success. Not every manager can be a generalist who can lead a project at any stage of development. Sometimes, those with the creative vision to launch products aren't the same managers with the operational skills to deliver and maintain product delivery quality day after day.

AN EMPATHETIC APPROACH

Hiring managers need to look beyond the immediate task of filling an opening with someone who just meets today's needs. Empathetic leaders take into consideration an employee's needs for growth and development, as well as the organization's future needs in a role as it grows and develops. By providing ongoing support, they give an employee the resources to succeed. And by adapting requirements as the situation evolves, they stay true to the organization's needs.

TIP #5:
UNLEASH HIDDEN POTENTIAL

"Leadership is unlocking people's potential to become better."
Bill Bradley, US Senator

"Potential is a priceless treasure, like gold. All of us have gold hidden within, but we have to dig to get it out."
Joyce Meyer, author and speaker

"A word of encouragement from a teacher to a child can change a life. A word of encouragement from a spouse can save a marriage. A word of encouragement from a leader can inspire a person to reach her potential."
John C. Maxwell, author

Do you have any employees who are limited to a role well beneath their capabilities? Are they hidden in plain sight? What would unleashing this potential do for the organization's culture, performance, and financial success? An underemployed friend recently shared her frustration at not being permitted to contribute at the level of which she is capable. Empathetic leaders go out of their way to learn about their team members hidden skills so that they can put individuals in positions where they can benefit themselves and the organization to the fullest.

Point of Reference
A recent national job satisfaction survey from the Society for Human Resources Management (SHRM) included a shocker. For the first time, "opportunities to use skills and abilities" displaced job security (63 percent to 61 percent) as the most important aspect of job satisfaction.

The bottom line: we want to be secure, but even more than that, we want to be *fulfilled* in our work. President Kennedy once defined happiness as "the full use of one's talents along lines of excellence." In this way, we all want to be happy by being all that we can be.

Recognize These People?

Do any of these folks work at your company?

- **MBA-educated hourly customer service rep** – She has fifteen years of prior professional experience, but when she makes process improvement suggestions, she's not taken seriously due to her position.
- **Non–degreed assistant manager** – The company is happy to have him supervising the day-to-day operations of a large branch, but when it comes to managing a high-visibility nationwide project, those are tacitly reserved for degreed professionals only.
- **Receptionist-playwright** – Did you know that your friendly receptionist spent a dozen years as a budget analyst and project manager for a major bank and, in her spare time, is a playwright who founded and leads her own nonprofit community theater group?

If so, you may have individuals who are vastly underemployed and underutilized.

Unleashing Potential

How would it improve your organization's performance, if:

- You sought out the MBA-educated customer service rep, let her know that you appreciate her process-improvement suggestions, want her to keep them coming, and encourage her to post for higher-skill positions in the company?

- You realize that you've advertised a management role for months without finding a candidate with the right fit of experience and culture. You loosen the degree requirements, focus on who can truly do the job, and invite the non-degreed assistant branch manager in for a serious interview and career- planning discussion.
- You're reorganizing a chronically underperforming department and are about to advertise for a project manager to lead the effort. Then you remember the receptionist's background and wonder if this is the sort of thing she has done in a past life. When she jumps at the opportunity and hits the ground running, you smile in satisfaction (and relief at finally solving the problem).

Where to Find This Information

With managers at all levels just as overwhelmed as their employees—having little time to think deeply about the latent skills, talents, and experience of their employees—the what-if above might strike some as unrealistic. But it's really not. It just takes a little time and effort.

Large organizations may have detailed "skills inventories" within their HR systems; see your HR department for details. In many organizations, though, this information can really only be obtained in the old-fashioned way, i.e., by the manager getting to know their employees, and having formal and informal career discussions with them, so that they know what they've done in the past and what they hope to do in the future. There is no substitute for one-to-one communication and getting to know your employees' professional hopes and dreams.

AN EMPATHETIC APPROACH

What shows more empathy than taking the time to get to know your employees' backgrounds and professional goals? Given the huge upside potential involved—being able to utilize and empower existing employees' talents and desires to the fullest—an empathetic leader, committed to digging a little deeper to see the answers that might be right in front of everyone, may be all it takes to improve the lives of the employees and the organization.

TIP #6:
PREPARE NEW MANAGERS

"I start with the premise that the function of leadership is to produce more leaders, not more followers."
Ralph Nader, activist

"The growth and development of people is the highest calling of leadership."
Harvey Firestone, industrialist

"Before you are a leader, success is all about growing yourself. When you become a leader, success is all about growing others."
Jack Welch, CEO, General Electric

I once worked with a senior leader who was considering promoting a longtime employee to a supervisory position for the first time. To help paint a picture of management for the employee, the executive drew up a list of "Things Managers *Are* and *Do*" and shared it with the prospective supervisor. It was a very good and thoughtful list, so I asked him if I might "steal" it, adding a few thoughts of my own.

Things Managers <u>Are</u>

- They are *genuine* (i.e., they know that admitting mistakes makes you human, not weak)
- They are *prudent* (i.e., they balance the needs of all concerned)
- They are *thoughtful* (i.e., they try to understand and consider the implications of their actions)
- They are *humble* (i.e., they seek collegial relationships and use power with great restraint)
- They are *hopeful* (i.e., they believe in others' potential and work to help them fulfill it)

Things Managers <u>Do</u>

- They *manage* (i.e., they take charge of situations, identifying solutions rather than complaining about problems)
- They *want* to manage (because they enjoy this type of work, not because of where it puts them on the corporate ladder)
- They *care about* and come to know their staff as individuals first, and coworkers second.
- They understand and respect that people have a life outside of work and try to plan thoughtfully to help their teams *balance business and personal responsibilities*
- They truly want their staff and coworkers to be successful, and they work to help them become so
- They see this role (helping others succeed) *as being equally important* as "doing their own job" because it *is* their job
- They actively demonstrate support by being available, teaching, and offering tools and resources where they reasonably can
- They continually seek *to learn and develop* themselves in order to become better managers
- They don't have to *win an argument* because they're the boss (i.e., they seek to let the best answer prevail, regardless of who has the best answer)
- They understand that they're not owed trust and loyalty merely because they're a manager; they *have to earn it* (day by day, action by action).

<u>AN EMPATHETIC APPROACH</u>

Empathetic leaders are purposeful, engaging, sincere, and thoughtful. They consider the needs of their employees and their organization before their own needs. If they model the behaviors and traits noted —and inculcate them in the managers on their teams—they will be serving their employees, organizations, and themselves, to the fullest.

TIP #7:
ASSESS THE COSTS AND BENEFITS
OF ROCK STARS AND ROLE PLAYERS

"A guy that's going to do all of the dirty work, that guy that is willing to defend anyone and do the little things and not really care about all of that other stuff.
I think every championship team needs that."
Draymond Green, NBA champion

"If we were all determined to play the first violin, we should never have an ensemble. Therefore, respect every musician in his proper place."
Robert Schumann, German composer

"Do not tolerate brilliant jerks. The cost to teamwork is too high."
Reed Hastings, CEO, Netflix

The passing of Apple's legendary leader, Steve Jobs, brought with it a flood of tributes from every corner. Many noted his amazing impact on the way we communicate, work, and entertain ourselves. At the same time, a portion noted the downside of Jobs' demanding nature that could often demean employees, with one article noting that his famously creative temperament simultaneously wrought "bullying, manipulation, and fear" within Apple (Gawker.com, 10/7/11). This is not unlike behavior that has been ascribed to Elon Musk, CEO of Tesla and Space-X, more recently.

Such "rock star" employees are present in many organizations. In these cases, managers need to assess whether the benefits of the rock star performer's gifts outweigh the emotional and other costs of their difficult behavior if they devolve into polarizing and sometimes even abusive figures. Let's look at two examples.

Example #1: The Creator/Destroyer

This highly-talented, highly-prolific employee is revered for their ability to consistently produce and innovate in ways that take the company's line of products and services to the next level. However, their egocentric nature can also play out as intellectual bullying, shutting down all lines of thinking not aligned with their own, and thus severely limiting the ability of other team members to work collaboratively.

In this way, they often destroy (in terms of culture) as much as they create in product. The opportunity cost of diminished collaboration may never be truly known, but the negative impact to culture has an undoubtedly lasting effect.

Example #2: High Potential/High Maintenance

An up-and-coming employee identified as "high potential" can provide a contagious energy, enthusiasm, and curiosity, creating an environment in which everyone stretches to grow and develop. Conversely, a high achiever of a different temperament may display an unwillingness to engage in grunt work that is inevitably part of most jobs, feeling it is a poor use of their time and talents. Where an "everyone pitches in" mentality is central to the company's culture, the high-potential's sense of superiority and entitlement can feed resentment in others and lead to contentious working relationships.

Another Option: A Championship Team of Role-Players

An alternative to the rock stars model is to construct a championship-caliber team of role-players. Looking to the sporting world for example, two recent World Series champions—the 2015 Kansas City Royals and the 2018 Boston Red Sox—followed such a model. Both the Royals and the Red Sox had highly talented players, to be sure, but none were rock stars in comparison to others in Major League Baseball. However, as the season and then playoffs played out, it became clear that from the first man in the lineup to the last, they had the strongest *teams* in the league.

Regardless of circumstances, each batter, pitcher, or player in the field seemed to execute their job perfectly every time. They played as a team and eagerly did the dirty work that was necessary for success—bunting runners over, hitting the cut-off man, getting ahead in the count, etc. In the end, they overpowered their opponents with relentless execution and took home the World Series trophy.

AN EMPATHETIC APPROACH

When the behavior of rock star employees begins to harm the organization, empathetic leaders recognize that the costs -- in the form of damaged morale, negative work environment, and a polarized culture -- may have exceeded the employee's benefits. Taking seriously the needs of all other team members, as well as recognizing the organization's need to maintain a healthy culture, the empathetic manager may wish to construct a team of strong role-players, instead.

This isn't to suggest settling for mediocre skills. Rather, it is to say that high-skill/low-maintenance role-players may benefit the organization much more in the long run than the supremely-talented-but-highly-costly rock star's contributions. You can win the World Series, so to speak, with either model. One is likely to be much more sustainable and beneficial over the long-term, though.

TIP #8:
REMEMBER THAT YOU'RE RECRUITING (AND RETAINING) THE WHOLE FAMILY

"Always treat your employees exactly as you want them to treat your best customers."
Stephen R. Covey, The 7 Habits of Highly Effective People

"Build relationships before you need them."
Tim Sanders, Yahoo executive

"Employees who believe that management is concerned about them as a whole person—not just an employee—are more productive, more satisfied, more fulfilled. Satisfied employees mean satisfied customers, which leads to profitability."
Anne M. Mulcahy, former CEO, Xerox

Recruiting is a difficult and time-consuming activity. As a manager, you're busy trying to run your team, department, division, etc., which has been made tougher by the departure of a valued member. While you're trying to help everyone pick up the slack, you're also working with your HR person or recruiter to define job specs, review résumés, and interview candidates—all in the hopes that in the end, you'll find a needle-in-the-haystack candidate who can walk right in and start making your lives easier from day one.

Empathetic leaders do all of that, and also take on one additional burden: carrying out the hiring in a way that treats all candidates with dignity and respect and makes it much easier for their families to support their work. Empathetic leaders remember that encouragement (or discouragement) shared by their employees' families goes a long way toward determining if the new employee stays, is engaged in their work, and performs well over the long-term.

Proper Care and Feeding of Candidates

In a busy, disruptive economic environment, niceties of ordinary recruiting behavior, such as getting back to candidates with feedback in a timely manner, can easily fall by the wayside. However, the truth, I believe, is that these aren't just niceties—they are business imperatives because they impact your employer brand. Most organizations zealously guard their customer brand, with obvious reason, as it is one of their most valuable assets. The employer brand, though, isn't always handled with as much care and forethought. It is never acceptable to fail to respond to *customers*, yet it is acceptable to many companies to do so with *candidates*.

Everyone wants to be an "employer of choice," where candidates are coming to you, versus having to beat the bushes to drum up applicants every time there's an opening. Some of this has to do with the strength of your technology, financial results, or your benefits, salaries, and culture. And some of it has to do with your reputation among candidates. With the increasing popularity of sites like Glassdoor.com, where candidates, employees, and former employers provide their assessments of the company, employer reputation is becoming more and more important in the war for talent.

Before deciding to apply, highly qualified candidates want to know what life is like at the company. This includes how candidates are treated during the interview process. The number one complaint of candidates on Glassdoor is that they received no word on their status after having interviewed or that they were misled or misinformed about the job during the interview. No one expects to get an offer from every company they interview with. However, everyone expects to find out in a timely manner if the company is still interested. It's as simple as that.

Adding Family into the Employer-Branding Equation

If your family is anything like mine, when someone is out of work or looking for a better job, *everyone* knows they are going for the interview ... everyone is praying, hoping, wishing for them ... and everyone is waiting for the results. Telling everyone you didn't get the job is bad enough. Telling them that you don't know if you got the job—that the company thought so little of you that they didn't even bother getting back to you—is far more embarrassing and damages the reputation of the company in the community and with the candidate's family and friends. Many people can take rejection or poor treatment in stride when it comes to themselves, but no one likes to see their spouse, child, or sibling suffer disrespectful treatment. It's a law of nature that mama bear and papa bear protect their cubs.

The converse is also true. If a candidate comes on board and you treat them well, their family remembers the positive experience and is much more likely to help the employee hang in there during any difficult times with the company that may occur in the future. You're making a very positive deposit into the emotional bank account, and one that will pay dividends for years to come.

AN EMPATHETIC APPROACH

Partner with your HR team to make sure that candidates are handled with as close to white-glove treatment as possible. Running HR isn't your job, of course, but you have a vested interest in how well they treat candidates. If HR knows white-glove candidate treatment is important to you as the hiring manager, it is much more likely they'll give the follow-up process the time and attention it deserves. It will pay off, as positive relations with the candidate (and hopefully, then the employee) will spread through the family and community and strengthen your employer brand.

TIP #9:
RECOGNIZE CONNECTORS AND LINCHPINS

"The whole is greater than the sum of its parts."
Aristotle, ancient Greek philosopher

Connector (n.)
a person or thing that links two or more things together

Linchpin (n.)
a person or thing vital to an enterprise or organization
www.oxforddictionaries.com

In any organization, there are people who bring—and hold—the team together. One type (call them the "linchpins"), fills key gaps in the team that, now, with their presence, is locked firmly together. The other type (call them the "connectors") delights in bringing disparate teammates, managers, vendors, and customers together, like matchmakers from days of yore. They serve as the company's informal "introducers-in-chief," if you will.

Empathetic leaders will see the value in—and actively seek out and support—both linchpins and connectors, recognizing that they make the individuals and the team as a whole stronger, more connected, and more aware of each other's gifts and talents.

Linchpins: Making the Team Stronger

An example of a linchpin is baseball Hall of Famer, the late Gary Carter. A power-hitting catcher for nineteen seasons, Carter served as a field general behind the plate, and his upbeat personality and strong will to win enabled him to be a leader off the field. In the many eulogies offered on his premature passing, there was constant reference to the role Carter played as the "last piece of the puzzle" when he was traded to the New York Mets in 1985, leading them to a World Series championship a year later.

Carter was recognized as the glue that held a very talented but undisciplined team together. His confidence behind the plate enabled him to patiently guide a young pitching staff through inevitable rough spots in their development. In the batter's box, his fierce will to win was exemplified in getting the crucial two-outs-in-the-bottom-of-the-ninth-with-no-one-on-base hit that started the Mets' miraculous game-winning rally in a contest known forever in New York sports lore simply as "Game Six."

His presence in the heart of the lineup and in the center of the baseball diamond reassured teammates on both offense and defense, grounding them in the belief that they had the talent and skill to overcome all obstacles and challenges. In this way, he served as the linchpin that helped his teammates join together to become more than the sum of the parts.

Connectors: Matchmakers, Includers, and Introducers

For several years, I worked with a colleague, Anna, who is brilliant in her ability to bring people together. A true expert in her field of study, Anna continually seeks out the best and the brightest in other fields and seeks to bring them into her realm to participate and contribute to the success of any project.

With very little fanfare, Anna regularly brings individuals into her projects in ways in which they can add the most value, expand their contacts, serve the client's best interests, and play to their strengths. While the connections might not seem obvious at first—e.g., when she brought me as an HR expert into a fundraising project she was conducting—teammates soon learn to trust her instincts. Anna has a knack for bringing someone into exactly the spot – and at exactly the time – when they can make the biggest impact. She is a true connector, and the individuals and the team are strengthened for it.

Counterpoint: Disconnectors

In contrast to both examples above, I once interviewed with the HR department of a Fortune 500 company where (strikingly) there seemed to be absolutely no connection (business, emotional, or otherwise) between any member of the HR team … so much so that the word "team" could scarcely be used.

This disconnect extended to the HR Vice-President, an otherwise affable and bright person who was (shockingly) proud to share that he had "no idea" what anyone on his team was doing at any point in time—nor did he see any reason to. Not surprisingly, it was one of the coldest and most sterile environments I had ever observed in an HR department. Wow, did that team ever need a connector and a linchpin!

AN EMPATHETIC APPROACH

Empathetic leaders recognize the role that linchpins and connectors play on their teams. While these aren't formal titles on the organization chart, they are often critical to success. When you are observing a team and feel that there is "just something missing," it will often be a lack of someone to tie everything together. Hiring or encouraging individuals who can serve as linchpins and connectors can put all the pieces together and make all the difference in the team's success and satisfaction.

CHAPTER 2
MANAGING THE TEAM

Once the majority of their team is in place, the empathetic leader will shift their attention to developing the people on their team—helping them enhance their skills, setting goals and objectives, and organizing the team for maximum growth, while navigating around any bumps in the road. It's all about seeing what will maximize the team's potential, and then providing resources to help get them where the they need to be.

As a preview, the tips and anecdotes shared in this chapter include:

- How to recognize when the team needs a jolt of confidence—and how to help give it to them
- Using performance reviews as an opportunity to strengthen relationships
- Ensuring that you're delegating in a way that builds trust with your team
- Letting the team know that you're rooting for their success
- Using Maslow's Hierarchy of Needs to understand and resolve performance difficulties
- Recognizing when promotions are warranted, and granting them in a way that builds employees' confidence and grows their skills and experience
- Being certain that you're asking things of your team that are within their capabilities

- Gaining perspective so that you can be sure that you're solving the right problem
- Knowing when it is time to reassign or say so long to team members—and having the courage and confidence to do so
- Using kindness and support to build the team's capacity

TIP #10:
BUILD CONFIDENCE

"Each time we face our fear, we gain strength, courage, and confidence in the doing."
Theodore Roosevelt, 26th U.S. President

"Trust yourself. You know more than you think you do."
Benjamin Spock, medical doctor, author

"Whatever course you decide upon, there is always someone to tell you that you are wrong. There are always difficulties arising which tempt you to believe that your critics are right. To map out a course of action and follow it to an end requires courage."
Ralph Waldo Emerson, poet

Part of a leader's job is to build up the confidence of employees in the organization—particularly those just starting out in their careers. A recent experience reminded me that sometimes we also need to build up the confidence of those who we often assume are *already* confident: executives and other accomplished professionals.

When Things Get Overwhelming

I once was asked to facilitate a two-day off-site planning meeting for a group of industry executives contemplating an ambitious project. Their aim was to develop a training and certification program that would become the recognized gold standard in their industry.

Working diligently in a very pleasant conference facility in the Arizona desert in early winter, the group soon had several whiteboards full of potential curriculum designs and course outlines spread around the boardroom. As the first day came to a close and we did a brief recap before dinner, I was quite struck by the group's reaction. As each person took in the array of courses and materials noted on the boards, they vocalized something I wasn't expecting: they felt overwhelmed.

The participants were all very accomplished in their field and prominent leaders in their respective organizations (all were CFOs or the equivalent). And yet, even for this group of senior leaders, the size of the task before them, laid out in visual form on the whiteboards, was somewhat daunting. "I'm not sure I'm qualified to teach even one of these courses," one person remarked quietly, spurring "me, too's" from the others.

Remedies: Breaking Tasks into Pieces

After I recovered from my surprise, I quickly moved forward with the first two tactics that came to mind:

- Breaking the larger tasks down into more manageable pieces
- Giving the group "permission" not to have to accomplish everything all in one fell swoop

Instead of looking at fifty individual courses, we grouped the courses into manageable "tracks," leaving the group breathing a little easier at the thought of designing ten groups of things, rather than fifty individual items. At the same time, I went back to the maxim that "Rome wasn't built in a day," and encouraged them not to feel they needed to teach everything they knew all at one time, as it would be as overwhelming for the students as it would be for the instructors. They could start small—i.e., building "phase one"—and go from there.

Lessons Learned

Those few days in the desert reminded me that we can build confidence, from the entry level to the boardroom, by reducing unnecessary pressure that might otherwise paralyze and overwhelm, and by breaking down complexity so that people can chip away, piece by piece, gaining strength one step at a time. This can be a healthy—and necessary—approach ... even with self-confident executives!

AN EMPATHETIC APPROACH

Never assume that even the most seasoned members of a team are fully comfortable with all their responsibilities and objectives. Taking the time to ask for their thoughts, and listening to any concerns, doubts, or fears they may have, provides the opportunity to help guide even the most senior and capable leaders.

TIP #11:
USE REVIEWS TO BUILD RELATIONSHIPS

"Appreciate everything your associates do for the business. Nothing else can quite substitute for a few well-chosen, well-timed, sincere words of praise. They're absolutely free and worth a fortune."
Sam Walton, founder, Walmart

"Good leaders make people feel that they're at the very heart of things, not at the periphery. Everyone feels that he or she makes a difference to the success of the organization. When that happens, people feel centered and that gives their work meaning."
Warren G. Bennis, leadership expert and author

Everyone wants to know where they stand with their manager and their company. Leaders that work hard to assess employee performance and give feedback regularly are doing an important part of their job as a manager. One aspect of the performance review process that is often overlooked, though, is to use the review discussion as an opportunity to build their relationship with the employee. This comes through candid dialogue not only about their performance, but about their professional aspirations and how they might achieve them.

The story below illustrates a time where the leader did a great job in writing the review but completely missed the relationship-building aspect that was right before her.

The Best of Times; The Worst of Times

Looking somewhat dejected on a Monday afternoon, a friend sat down beside me, handed me a copy of his performance review, and asked me to read it. Seeing his demeanor, I was expecting to find nasty comments, absurdly low rating, or other classic performance review-related issues.

As I read through what he handed me, though, what I saw was clearly a very positive review, with strong compliments—even ending with a handwritten note from his boss thanking him for his service and looking forward to even greater success in the coming year, which was a nice touch.

"I'm a little confused," I told him. "This is a *great* review."

"It is," he replied.

"It looks your boss has done just about everything we would teach in a performance management class. She used several specific examples of your accomplishments, and she included feedback from your colleagues and clients. She set new goals for next year ... and she even approved the professional development plan that you proposed," I suggested hopefully.

"I know," he said, still looking like Eeyore from *Winnie the Pooh*.

"So why the long face?" I finally asked.

He sighed and said, "I'm glad she wrote the things that she did, but I don't know how she did it. I mean, *she never talked to me voluntarily once* the whole year (other than "hello" and "goodbye"), not even to stop by for a minute to see how things were going—and I work twelve feet from her office. To make matters worse, she left the review on my desk when I was out last Friday. She didn't ask to meet with me to discuss things. It feels like, as far as she is concerned, that's the end of that for another year."

And there you have it: *assessment* without *relationship*. A morale killer, indeed.

Perspective

My friend's boss had done (almost) everything right in compiling his review. But she forgot just one thing. Yes, performance reviews are designed to let both the company and the employee have a clear, common understanding of how the employee performed during the year, and facts and examples need to be recorded. Yes, evaluations are places for fine-tuning goals and providing professional development guidance for the future. But they are also about building relationships and creating a two-way dialogue about the employee's performance, goals, and professional aspirations.

Ideally, a performance review represents a summary of all the coaching and check-in conversations (formal and informal) that the employee and manager have had over the year. Much to her credit, my friend's manager recorded the *facts* ... but she missed the *relationship* part entirely. Her employee wanted to know not only that his boss was paying attention, but that she cared enough about him to occasionally spend a few minutes discussing his path forward at different points throughout the year.

Mutual Responsibility for the Relationship

I didn't want to add to my friend's pain at the time, of course, but as a confidante, I should have asked if he checked in with his boss during the year, or requested time on her calendar to sit down and chat, to get her views on his projects and where he was heading, etc.

Relationships go both ways, and as professionals, we share the burden of speaking up and asking for feedback if we're not getting the response, coaching, or direction that we're looking for. Our bosses are busy, too, and a mutually trusting and respectful relationship requires both sides to reach out when needed.

AN EMPATHETIC APPROACH

As leaders, we need to remember that employees want to know that their bosses are not only paying attention to what they do but that they also value us as individuals. For most of us, this means maintaining at least a semi-regular dialogue (whether in person, on the phone, or through Skype, or Slack, or email) throughout the year. Going the extra mile to engage our employees as individuals during the year takes a little effort, but it pays off by strengthening working relationships and avoiding unnecessary misunderstandings which can wipe out all the otherwise well-intentioned work that manager and employee do throughout the year.

TIP #12:
DELEGATE TO BUILD TRUST
AND ENGAGEMENT

*"The beauty of empowering others is that your own power
is not diminished in the process."*
Barbara Coloroso, speaker, author, advocate

*"I'm going from doing all of the work to having to delegate the work—
which is almost harder for me than doing the work myself.
I'm a lousy delegator, but I'm learning."*
Alton Brown, celebrity chef

*"When you delegate tasks, you create followers. When you delegate
authority, you create leaders."*
Craig Groeschel, pastor

*"If you want to do a few small things right, do them yourself. If you want to
do great things and make a big impact, learn to delegate."*
John C. Maxwell, management expert, author

A recent reality TV show reaffirmed an important lesson for me about managing: everyone wants their boss to trust them, and there's nothing like delegation to show trust. When trust isn't present, it can crush an employee's spirit and performance.

Restaurant Impossible
On the Food Network show, *Restaurant Impossible*, chef Robert Irvine works with once-thriving and now-floundering restaurants to turn them around. Each episode features business lessons about failing to listen to customers, degrading quality standards, and not

56

keeping up with industry trends—and the stories are often heartbreaking (i.e., owners who have put their lives into an establishment, only to see their dreams slip away slowly as business declines and debts mount).

One episode told the story of a once-successful family steakhouse that had lost its way with the husband-and-wife ownership team working more and more hours and seeing fewer and fewer customers. Chef Irvine helped the husband see that his need for control was one of the central problems in the operation.

Example: The owner spent hours each day portioning out the meat into eight-ounce filets, twelve-ounce chops, etc. When asked why he couldn't have his chefs do this as part of their daily routine, he replied: "Because *I* have to do it." When asked how long his chefs had been with him, his answer was stunning: "twenty-five years each."

Twenty-five years and he didn't even trust his chefs to trim meat! Remarkable. Not surprisingly, they weren't empowered to come up with daily specials, either. However, when Chef Irvine convinced the owner to let the chefs trim the meat just once, they did so perfectly … on the first try. When they were asked to create a daily special, their passion, pride, and energy practically jumped through the screen, completely changing their entire demeanor—and the atmosphere of the restaurant, along with it.

Learn from My Experience: Don't Be the Bottleneck

Sometimes we fail to delegate because we feel no one else can do the task as well as us or because we gain satisfaction (and/or security) from the task. In most cases, this gets in the way of a team's performance by communicating a lack of trust that decimates motivation. Other times, we're think we're "helping" when we're simply setting ourselves up as a bottleneck.

This was the case early in my career. I was managing a small team of very capable professionals charged with handling all the HR issues around mergers and acquisitions. I spent much of my time and energy coaching and mentoring the team (which was good). Unfortunately, I decided to keep a few tasks for myself. With so much of my focus on helping the team, it inevitably turned out that my tasks were last to be completed. Essentially, I became the bottleneck. The team was more than capable, and there was no reason that I had to hang onto these tasks. If I had simply delegated all the tasks and focused solely on coaching, coordinating, and providing overall direction, we would have been much better off.

AN EMPATHETIC APPROACH
Don't be the manager who doesn't trust his chefs to trim meat after twenty-five years. (Can you imagine how that made them feel?) Be the leader who empowers your team and guides them to deliver a delicious dining (or business) experience for everyone involved.

TIP #13:
ENGAGE ALL AND ROOT
FOR THEIR SUCCESS

*"As we look ahead into the next century, leaders will be those
who empower others."*
Bill Gates, founder of Microsoft

*"Our chief want is someone who will inspire us to be what
we know we could be."*
Ralph Waldo Emerson, poet

"Instruction does much, but encouragement everything."
Johann Wolfgang von Goethe, German writer and statesman

Welcoming Contributions from All

Attending Mass in my parent's parish one Sunday, I observed
something that I hadn't seen before. When it came time for the
collection, the pastor (an upbeat, encouraging man) invited all the
children in attendance to bring their dimes and dollars to a special jar
he had set up to collect donations for the poor. The gesture not only
permitted them to expend some of their youthful energy by running
down the aisle, but also allowed even the smallest members of the
congregation to contribute.

One only needed to see the smiles on their faces as they ran back to
their parents to know the many silent lessons that were being
inculcated in them that day—such as a sense of contribution, and a
sense of being needed and valued.

Rooting for Them

Just as sports fans root for their teams, empathetic leaders root for those in their charge. This isn't limited to the youngest or newest members of the team (as above) but it extends to executives, as well.

As a young HR person, I recall helping my boss (president of a twenty-five-million-dollar business unit at the time) prepare for an important presentation at corporate headquarters. Though a naturally charismatic personality with a strong grasp on the facts and plans that she'd be presenting, she was nevertheless a bit nervous stepping into this arena. As I recall, she lost a bit of sleep preparing and revising her transparencies (in the days before PowerPoint).

Upon my boss' return from her trip, we discussed how the presentation went. I vividly recall her broad smile in reply. "I was a little nervous starting off. But then I looked down and I saw Carter (our CEO) sitting in the front row. He was smiling up at me with this look on his face that just told me how much he was rooting for me to do well. Once I saw that, I was fine and I sailed through the rest of the presentation."

AN EMPATHETIC APPROACH

Empathetic leaders remember that:

1. Everyone on our team wants to participate and contribute. It's our job as leaders to give them the opportunity to do so in meaningful, productive ways.
2. Everyone needs encouragement, including the most senior amongst us. If we can keep these simple notions in mind, we'll be leading with empathy, and drawing the most out of our teams.

TIP #14:
REPAIR RELATIONSHIPS
THROUGH SERVICE

"We can become stronger at the broken places."
Ernest Hemingway, A Farewell to Arms

"Hold no grudges and practice forgiveness. This is the key
to having peace in all your relationships."
Dr. Wayne Dyer, author, speaker

At dinner during an off-site sales meeting, the conversation was lively, the atmosphere cozy, and the mood light as someone rose with glass in hand. "I'd like to offer a toast to Patty for the terrific way that she has supported us this past year." Looking over the clinking of glasses and the round of warm congratulations sat an embarrassed but clearly gratified Patty. This simple scene represented the culmination of a years-long journey to rebuild tattered relations between the sales and marketing teams—and therein lies our story.

The Backstory
For more than a decade, relations between sales and marketing in this small organization had been frayed, sometimes to the breaking point. This reflected in large part the contentious relationship between the heads of both groups. Words like *toxic, angry, skeptical, uncommunicative, antagonistic,* and the like could be used to describe the tone between the groups at various points. How did things move from this polarized state to the happy dinner scene above? It took a series of steady, persistent actions over the course of years.

Breaking Down Barriers

Several steps—some intentional, some happenstance—served to break the logjam and help move the relationship between the groups forward.

- **Change in Players** – The first key event was the departure of the prior marketing head. The hard feelings between herself and the sales head had become so entrenched that no progress would have been likely without some change in the principals.

- **Determination** – Upon assuming his position, the new marketing leader (Sean) assigned a different member of his team (Patty) to be the direct liaison with the sales team. Patty had lived through the past wars and came into the role determined to turn things around. She made it her mission to repair and restore the relationship.

- **Establishing Credibility** – Patty's approach wasn't to make big promises regarding planned improvements. Rather, she felt what she needed to do in her interactions with the sales team was ask questions, fulfill their requests quickly with as little drama as possible, and over time, begin to influence the direction of the work by inserting her ideas as they became more comfortable that she was meeting their needs and could be counted on. It was, it turned out, an excellent plan.

- **Moving from Order-Taker to Partner** – The final step in the transformation occurred over the course of two semiannual sales team planning meetings. During the summer meeting, Patty presented a brief status report. By the time of the winter meeting six months later, the sales manager invited her to facilitate a session with the team regarding their sales goals and how she could help fulfill them.

The culmination of this dialogue brought the groups to the celebratory dinner and the toast was a sign of her acceptance as a partner to the sales team. It was a long journey … but one that thereafter proceeded much more collaboratively than would have been conceivable at the outset.

AN EMPATHETIC APPROACH

Where interpersonal or interdepartmental relationships have broken down, taking some of the steps that Patty followed may help empathetic leaders restore tattered working relationships. Seeking to understand and serve the other's needs without asserting your own agenda helps to establish credibility and trust—which serves as the basis for a healthy working relationship from that moment forward.

TIP #15:
REMEMBER MASLOW WHEN
SOLVING PROBLEMS

"One can choose to go back toward safety or forward toward growth. Growth must be chosen again and again; fear must be overcome again and again."

"A musician must make music, an artist must paint, a poet must write, if he is to be ultimately at peace with himself. What a man can be, he must be."

"What is necessary to change a person is to change his awareness of himself."
Abraham Maslow, psychologist, writer

One day, as I was working with a manager trying to help an employee who seemed to be cracking under various pressures, the light bulb went on for me. There we were, trying to fix what appeared to be a performance problem, never recognizing that the real issue was something far different. All I could think to say was, "Maslow was right."

Maslow Was Right
Abraham Maslow was a psychologist who, in the 1950s, published a famous article proposing a "Hierarchy of Needs." He suggested that human behavior progressed through sequential (or hierarchical) needs, as detailed in his famous pyramid, illustrated below. His theory proposed that one doesn't progress to a higher-level need until the lower-level need is satisfied (e.g., you aren't going to be focused on "being all you can be" if you're hungry, homeless, or otherwise unsafe).

Maslow's Hierarchy of Needs

(image from www.simplypsychology.org)

While I had known about the Maslow's hierarchy for more than twenty-five years, the truth of it finally hit me like a ton of bricks. Here we were trying to help someone self-actualize his behavior (i.e., guiding him to perform at the highest level) when he was actually struggling for survival in many ways (i.e., attending to lower-level safety and security needs).

It turned out that the employee was coming off his second divorce, adjusting to a new city, struggling with caring for aging parents long-distance, and trying to resolve significant financial pressures stemming from all the above. What chance in the world was there that he was going to focus on "being all he could be" at his job at this moment? He was just trying to survive, day to day. I should have seen that sooner. Much sooner.

Moving Toward an Answer

This employee's stresses weren't much different from those many employees bring into the workplace every day. By not recognizing this, managers and HR people can end up trying to solve the wrong problem, often making things worse by adding new and unnecessary pressures to their employees' work lives.

A recent study indicated that:

- Ninety-two percent of employees report that personal problems decrease their productivity at least temporarily
- Forty percent of absenteeism is due to depression
- Personal and interpersonal problems cause sixty-five to eighty-five percent of involuntary terminations.

While I believe heartily in having empathy in all things, I'm not one who believes that an employer is best positioned to try to solve an employee's personal problems. The employer isn't a psychologist, social worker, pastor, etc. Yet there is surely something meaningful that we as leaders can still do to help.

Resolution

The happy ending to this story is that, on his own, the employee decided to enter counseling to help manage the ongoing stresses in his life, supported, in part, by the company's EAP (Employee Assistance Program). In addition, his manager actively worked with him on managing stress at work by timing due dates and planning workloads differently than they had in the past. Perhaps a return to self-actualization discussions might be possible in the future, as the employee regained his personal footing. For now, though, the goal was to re-stabilize his situation and get him back to solid performance, then build from there.

AN EMPATHETIC APPROACH

Stepping back and assessing performance issues in the light of Maslow's hierarchy may help an empathetic leader determine whether their agenda for the situation matches what the employee is capable of at that time. Working from this perspective, we were able to start putting in place the conditions that made higher-level discussions with the employee more feasible in the future – avoiding the need to act precipitously in the moment and allowing time to discern reasonable actions and re-set appropriate incremental goals and expectations going forward.

TIP #16:
PROMOTIONS CAN CHANGE LIVES

"Stay away from people who belittle your ambitions. Small people always do that, but the really great make you believe that you, too, can become great."
Mark Twain, author, humorist

"There is no exercise better for the heart than reaching down and lifting people up."
John Holmes, author, US Army veteran

Promotion (v.)
1. activity that supports or provides active encouragement for the furtherance of a cause, venture, or aim
2. raising up someone to a higher position
Source: dictionary.com

When a close colleague, Andrea, received a well-deserved promotion, I was thrilled for her and her manager. I believe that purposeful promotions—recognizing and "raising people up" in the very best sense of the term—have the power to change careers and lives.

Why Promotions Matter
It's always nice to get praise and recognition, of course. But I find that when done thoughtfully, it can be much more than a "nice to have" or a brief shot-in-the-arm for morale purposes. In Andrea's case, the promotion:

- Showed her that she and her contributions were valued by the organization

- Gave her increased standing and confidence to interact with clients, colleagues, and vendors on a more equal footing as professional peers
- Changed her own thinking about what her career might hold in store and what possibilities could become realities for her
- Increased her already strong appreciation for her manager, knowing that he had gone to bat for her when he didn't have to
- Set her up for other jobs (inside and outside the company) for which holding her new title/level was an unstated (but very real) requirement.

In the manager's case, the promotion demonstrated he was:
- Someone who recognized the good work of his team members in meaningful ways
- Someone who promoted and advocated for (rather than being threatened by) his team members
- Worthy of his team members' trust.

A Counter-Example

Unfortunately, I've seen many managers who've taken the opposite tack and are threatened by their employees' success, who (more commonly) lack awareness or consideration for their employees' needs, or who don't see employee advocacy and advancement as one of their key responsibilities as managers.

I once supported a senior manager who couldn't be persuaded that a very bright analyst deserved a promotion from "Analyst I" to "Analyst II" (a very minor move in our compensation system at the time). The VP's reasoning was, "If I give her that promotion, she's just going to take the higher salary and stop producing." It was disheartening to hear that she believed someone who had demonstrated intelligence, consistency, and strong performance over

TIP #17:
EXPECT THE RIGHT THINGS
OF EMPLOYEES

"If you align expectations with reality, you will never be disappointed."
Terrell Owens, NFL Hall of Famer

"Expectations are dangerous when they are both too high and unformed."
Lionel Shriver, author

"Being a great boss is challenging people in the right way. Leading, not managing. Supporting them by giving them both a platform they can count on and expectations they can stretch for."
Seth Godin, marketing expert, entrepreneur

As the economy becomes ever more global and every industry becomes increasingly competitive, managers and employees are continually asked to "do more with less." Taken to the extreme, when employees are forced to run beyond capacity for too long with insufficient backup or relief, this often results in burned-out managers, demoralized employees, declining product quality, disenchanted customers, and vanishing profits.

Similar negative results can occur where employees are asked to do *the wrong things*—i.e., tasks for which they are unskilled, untrained, or ill-suited. I believe that this happens more often than we might expect, though it is often misdiagnosed as the employee having "limitations," experiencing declining performance, or "no longer being a good fit"—though none of these labels may necessarily truly fit the situation.

The Discouraged Sales Manager

A good friend, David, is a senior manager with responsibility for a team of outside sales representatives. Over the course of several months, David became increasingly frustrated with his team not due to poor sales results, but rather, due to the team's failure to think "strategically."

Example: When David asked his team to plan next quarter's sales meeting, they set about doing so quite efficiently, but without ever contemplating the goal or broader purpose of the meeting, ultimately planning an agenda that missed the mark and required considerable reworking on David's part.

A Question of Skills, Strengths, and Attributes

As David related this story, I reflected on similar frustrations he has expressed in the past. It struck me that the stories all had a common theme: he was looking for a strategy from them (i.e., defining what the group needed to accomplish in the meeting), but he was consistently getting "tactics" (e.g., "First, book the hotel. Next, identify a guest speaker.") Nothing that was done was incorrect or inappropriate; it just wasn't what he was really looking for.

The core issue was a misalignment of skills and expectations.

- The sales reps kept trying to do what they were good at—executing tactics to complete the task before them. That was how they were wired and that was what they are good at.
- David was asking them to step back and think about the big picture—i.e., discerning *why* they were approaching certain clients and markets, and considering whether other potential markets might be fertile ground.
- They weren't trained—or naturally inclined—to think this way, so they didn't. Thus, the misalignment of expectations and skills.

Why the Disconnect?

I suggested to David that the core problem might be he was asking them to serve in a role that didn't play to their natural strengths, inclinations, or training. No rep was underperforming in their actual job (closing sales), just in the job he wished they might do (managing a team, charting a course, etc.). Upon reflection, he agreed. He didn't necessarily feel any better about the situation, but he now understood the situation and could adjust his expectations accordingly.

AN EMPATHETIC APPROACH

When you are disappointed in someone's performance, it is worthwhile, as an empathetic leader, to examine whether what you are asking them to do aligns with their skills, training, and natural abilities. If the answer is no, any number of solutions may be possible. By defining the problem from this perspective, you'll avoid misdiagnosing the issue, reduce the anxiety of all concerned, and be well on your way to identifying a positive solution.

TIP #18:
STEP BACK TO SOLVE
THE RIGHT PROBLEM

"We cannot solve our problems with the same thinking we used when we created them."
Albert Einstein, physicist

"Solving problems means listening."
Sir Richard Branson, entrepreneur

"You can increase your problem-solving skills by honing your question-asking ability."
Michael J. Gelb, author

"I'm a big believer in lessons learned. Constantly with the team we go over, why? Why? Why? The only bad mistake is a mistake you don't learn from."
Ginny Rommety, CEO, IBM

It is said that if you stand too close to something (either physically or emotionally), you're bound to miss the big picture. For instance, you need to step back from a Monet or other Impressionist painting to see the full picture; if you stand too close, you get lost in what looks like a jumble of dots and colors.

Applying this in a corporate context is tricky when companies operate at internet speed and managers feel compelled to solve all problems immediately, not allowing themselves time to first step back and examine what needs solving in the first place. In these cases, it is important for empathetic leaders to take a breath to consider the issue more broadly.

Example of Solving the Wrong Problem: XYZ vs. ABC

The following example comes from a leadership team meeting reviewing a company's finances:

CFO: "The XYZ line of business is no longer profitable for us. We're losing money every time we perform the service."

Leadership Team Member: "But we really love the XYZ business; it's what we're all about."

Another Team Member (eagerly): "I have an idea. Maybe we can get more XYZ business by doing …."

Other Participants (chiming in with enthusiasm): "That's a great idea! Or maybe we could …"

CFO: "If we book more XYZ services, we're going to be more unprofitable. However, the good news is that the ABC service we developed last year is highly profitable for us. We should really put our efforts into building up ABC and phasing out XYZ."

Team Member: "But we don't really care about the ABC line. Maybe we could generate more XYZ business by …"

CFO: Sigh.

The next twenty minutes of the meeting went on in a similar vein.

Example #2: Reducing Duties Instead of Paying an Appropriate Salary

I had a young friend, Hal, who served as chief of staff for Sara, the head of an important business line in the company. Hal and Sara worked very well together until the topic of Hal's salary came up, a year into his role supporting Sara.

In approaching Sara about a salary increase, Hal led with a review of all the extra hours, energy, and effort he had put into the role over the past year and provided realistic comparisons to similar positions in the local marketplace. Sara was quite startled by this, and over the course of several conversations, the interactions between the two became contentious—wholly different from all their other work together.

At one point, Sara, seizing on Hal's statement about working extra hours, started exploring how to off-load some of Hal's duties to others – so that his workload would be more in line with his current salary. However, Hal loved the breadth and depth of his work, and wasn't eager to off-load responsibilities that he enjoyed and was good at. He wasn't seeking to lessen his hours; rather, he was just seeking to be paid what (in his view) was a fair salary in the marketplace.

The stalemate continued for many months, with each not quite hearing what the other was saying.

AN EMPATHETIC APPROACH

In the first example, it would have been more impactful for the CFO to immediately acknowledge the place that the iconic but unprofitable XYZ product line had in the company's heart. With the emotions out of the way, the team might have been able to hear his solution with less resistance and hostility or could have tried to solve for the right problem (finding ways to make XYZ profitable, not just selling more of the unprofitable version). By not acknowledging concerns and allowing for only one solution (building up the profitable-but-unloved ABC product), the CFO inadvertently launched the team into solving the wrong problem.

In the second example, if Sara could have shared with Hal *why* she was resistant to increasing his salary (whether due to budget limitations, unspoken concerns about his work, or other unstated reasons), he could have addressed those concerns rather than sending them down paths (such as reducing his hours or responsibilities) that neither of them was really seeking.

In both cases, taking the time to step back, ask why, and acknowledge and explore feelings would have helped avoid an endless loop of hurt feelings and trying to solve the wrong problem.

TIP #19:
HAVE THE COURAGE TO
"COUNSEL OUT"

"My advice on firing is simple: Treat that person the same way you'd want to be treated if you were in that situation. They're still a good person, just not the right fit. So how do you help them move on in a productive way that allows them to maintain their dignity?"
Mary Barra, CEO, General Motors

"It's not the people you fire who make your life miserable. It's the people you don't."
Dick Grote, Discipline Without Punishment

"Firing is not something you do to someone: firing is something you do for someone."
Larry Winget, motivational speaker

"The single biggest lesson I learned was when a hire isn't working out, fire them fast. My biggest mistakes, and where I've seen the worst results, were when I gave someone too many chances, or let a situation drift on for too long because I couldn't bring myself to terminate it."
Cindy Gallop, UK advertising executive

"So many amazing opportunities arise when a chapter of our life ends. When we resign from a job that we weren't happy in, or even get fired, it's actually a blessing because a better experience is waiting to happen. It's all about perspective."
Miya Yamanouchi, author

One of the most enjoyable parts of leadership is hiring someone who brings great energy, new and vital skills, and is a great fit with a company's culture. The flip side of this is that, for most leaders, helping individuals transition involuntarily out of an organization—even where they are clearly not in a position where they can contribute effectively—is one of the hardest and most heart-wrenching part of the job.

Firing (or exiting, terminating, counseling out, or whatever the latest euphemism of the day may be) takes courage and steadfastness of purpose. In the end, I would submit that, where warranted, firing is ultimately the most compassionate thing that an empathetic leader can do, freeing someone to pursue their greater purpose for the benefit of the team, the organization, and the individual themselves.

Counseling Out

Sometimes helping someone exit the organization with dignity takes only a few gentle nudges and quiet conversations; other times, considerably more force is required. The following are a few common situations from my own career where I helped counsel out someone … or wished that I had:

- **Not a Manager** – The middle manager who hated managing (which was felt acutely by her people) but who lit up like a Christmas tree when she talked about her former role as an individual contributor. She was an expert in her field and enjoyed and excelled at her job before she was promoted to management.
- **Not Aligned with New Operating Needs** – The longtime branch manager who could learn and adapt to the new systems and processes being implemented … but who didn't want to. While his boss was around, he was fully compliant and got the job done in the new way. When the boss was away, however, he immediately reverted back to his prior

methods, confusing his team as to whether the new methods really were in place, or not.

- **Not Aligned with Culture** – The reserved scientist who joined a shoot-from-the-hip employer. While he was an expert in the process the company wanted to implement, his academic demeanor and passive work style never enabled him to gain credibility with the rough-and-tumble team on the floor. Even though the company culture was changing to be more scientific and process-oriented, it was never going to evolve quickly enough to where the scientist would be comfortable or gain the personal credibility to get the team on-board with real and lasting process change in his field.

- **Not a Salesperson** – The high-energy, salt-of-the-earth, naturally charismatic operations leader who had it in her heart to pursue a sales role but who, surprisingly, struggled mightily at sales. As it turned out, her passion was *serving* people, not *selling* to them. Fortunately, right before the situation came to a head, an opportunity in major account support opened up, where she proved to be a perfect fit.

- **Not a Go-Getter** – The naturally talented, commissioned salesperson who was great at establishing rapport with customers but who didn't have the drive to keep increasing his sales. Despite constant "sticks and carrots" designed to motivate him, he always reverted to his comfort zone, to the exasperation of the succession of sales leaders assigned to coach him. You can't coach desire, of course.

Imagine what a difference it would have made in the lives of all these individuals if they had been in roles that played to their true strengths and passions, rather than getting stuck in the wrong roles or industries, often until it was too late, or they were too paralyzed to act on their own. And, what a difference it would have made to those around them not to have had to suffer under poor leadership or having to work harder to make up for underperforming coworkers.

A Personal Perspective

When I'm asked why I got into human resources, I relate back to observing my father's experiences as a manager in a county agency. Dad was a good manager, and he would often be asked to go straighten out previously poorly performing units—which he usually was able to do in short order. The only problem was when he would run into a poorly-performing, toxic, but "unfireable" employee in one of his new units.

Under agency regulations, it took months if not years to terminate employees with even the most egregious performance issues—an arduous process that few had the heart to undertake. I saw what a demoralizing effect this circumstance had on him and, I'm sure, the other hard-working employees who were forced to take up the slack for the underperforming employee who suffered through the employee's toxic behavior in silence. All of this is to say nothing, of course, about the damage done to the agency's clients by the employee's negligence or disregard.

It was clear to see that what was required was a manager (in this case, my dad) or an HR person (or both) to have the courage and stamina to exit this person from the organization. My dad did this, to everyone's thanks and benefit -- but it took more of a toll on him than was necessary, for sure.

Understanding this as an adolescent, I vowed then to do my part to right this wrong, as it were. If I couldn't help my dad's situation (he is now long retired), then at least I could stand up and do the right thing to protect other employees and organizations (and their customers) from having to suffer needlessly because someone lacked the courage to act.

Courage and Compassion

While it may not sound very empathetic to suggest firing someone, I believe that, when warranted, termination is an act of both courage and compassion.

- **Courage** – what leaders need when the situation calls for letting the employee go now, rather than waiting for the fourth or fifth or tenth incident of bad behavior
- **Compassion** – what leaders feel for those subjected to the negative effects of such employees

I'm not suggesting that we terminated employees rashly, improperly, or in violation of policy, of course. I am suggesting, though, that we all have chronic underperformers and "bad behavers" in our organizations who go unaddressed due to leaders shying away from having difficult conversations and making tough decisions—and that needs to be addressed.

AN EMPATHETIC APPROACH

Out of compassion for their team members, empathetic managers who take a stand and truly do the right thing for their organization should be congratulated and supported. Instead of finding reasons for endless documentation or further procrastination, they should be supported in letting the employee go with courage, compassion, and confidence.

With regard to the employee themselves, an empathetic leader understands that no one wants to be bad at their job, or to be stuck in a field or a role that they have no passion for. Let us have the courage to help get them out of the wrong job (or organization) … and help guide them to the right job (or organization), so that all may benefit.

TIP #20:
UNLEASH PRODUCTIVITY THROUGH EMPATHY

"Kind words can be short and easy to speak but their echoes are truly endless."
St. Mother Teresa of Calcutta

"Kindness is gladdening the hearts of those who are traveling the dark journey with us."
Henri-Frederic Amiel, Swiss philosopher

"There are scores of people waiting for someone just like us to come along; people who will appreciate our compassion, our encouragement, who will need our unique talents. Someone who will live a happier life merely because we took the time to share what we had to give."
Leo Buscaglia, author and speaker

As the calendar turns toward the holidays every year, we often give great thought to the gifts we will give and receive. What if you could give your team a simple gift at any time of the year that could cause a giant leap in their performance and raise their state of mind?

The Power of One

Even the most determined among us tend to get discouraged or overwhelmed when our to-do list gets too long. But what if we had only one task to concentrate on for the moment? What if we identified one thing that would really make a difference in our work lives (and maybe our personal lives, too), and in the life of the organization, and then saw that one thing through to completion? What if we did this for ourselves and for our team?

The Manager's Speech

What if when you walked into the office on Monday morning, you called everyone together and said something like this:

"Welcome back, everyone. I hope that you enjoyed a wonderful weekend of family, friends, and relaxation. Before we dash headlong into the responsibilities of the week, there is something I want to talk with you about: gift-giving.

"I know that we put a lot of time and energy into giving gifts during the holidays and on special occasions. Today, on this ordinary day, I want you to give yourself a gift. Actually, it will be a gift to your coworkers, the company, and our customers, as well.

"I know that there's probably at least one thing that keeps getting shoved to the bottom of our priority lists that nags at us—and that if we did it, we would feel a lot better. Things like:

- Having a heart-to-heart talk with the coworker who offended us six months ago and who we've been trying to avoid ever since
- Forgiving the client who seems to complain about every little thing and whose emails and calls we return more slowly and less eagerly than others
- Gathering up the courage to ask to attend the training course that seems scary but which you know will take your skills and your career to the next level
- Just taking an hour or two to attend to your own needs— cleaning up your files, deleting old emails, catching up on the stack of industry magazines that you think probably

contain some neat suggestions to help your work, if you only had the time to read them.

"Do yourself, and the organization, a great favor by taking the time to do just one of those things today. It might be the best gift you've ever given or received at work."

Results

If everyone on your team took up this challenge, what would it do to:

- **Performance and Efficiency** – by removing roadblocks and resentments that are silently holding people back
- **Customer Service** – turning a "problem client" into a fiercely loyal one, to say nothing of the impact on your Net Promoter Score (NPS)
- **Morale and Engagement** – helping employees feel that they are progressing rather than stagnating in their careers, and that they are working for a person and a firm that values and invests in their development
- **Enthusiasm and Satisfaction** – helping your team feel that they are organized enough to do their jobs in forty hours instead of being scattered and rundown for fifty-plus hours.

Wouldn't that be a great speech to give? What's standing in the way?

AN EMPATHETIC APPROACH

As empathetic leaders, we know that there are any number of roadblocks hampering employee performance on a daily basis—yet, we so seldom take the time to address them in ways that free up employees to do their best work for the organization, its customers, and their colleagues. By giving our team members this "assignment," we're potentially unleashing untold productivity and performance, to say nothing of increasing retention, enhancing engagement, and changing lives. We'll be speaking to their needs, perhaps in ways and on topics that they've been trying to engage us on forever. How powerful is that?

CHAPTER 3
DEVELOPING YOUR CULTURE

With their team in place, empathetic managers set about building and maintaining a culture that will engage, support, challenge, inspire, and retain talented employees. This is a culture built around the company's core values, most commonly including mutual respect, inclusion, candor, dedication, and openness to change, growth, and development.

Tips covered in this chapter include:

- Recognizing and celebrating behaviors and employees that support your mission and culture
- Taking employees seriously, and hearing out their concerns with sincerity and caring
- Realizing when special things are happening in the organization that go beyond standard operating procedure, and responding to the moment with confidence
- Remembering that change is never easy, and employees need to hear and understand pending changes multiple times before absorbing them fully
- Going the extra mile to seek out those who will go beyond the "echo chamber" and tell you the truth, whether you want to hear it or not

- Understanding when self-inflicted wounds have sent the team into a downward spiral—and knowing how to reverse the flow
- Recognizing the burdens that employees' families bear and the key support roles that they play, and reaching out in ways that earn their trust and confidence
- Assessing interpersonal and group dynamics within the team, and determining if team-building is needed, or whether other underlying causes and concerns are at play

TIP #21:
CELEBRATE THE RIGHT HEROES

"Day after day, ordinary people become heroes through extraordinary and selfless actions to help their neighbors."
Sylvia Mathews Burwell, President, American University

"It is unwise to be too sure of one's own wisdom. It is healthy to be reminded that the strongest might weaken and the wisest might err."
Mahatma Gandhi

"When a manager recognizes an employee's behavior, personally and sincerely, both feel proud, gratified, and happy. There's a human connection that transcends the immediate culture to create a shared bond. The power of this bond is stronger than you might think; indeed, it's the power that holds together great organizational cultures."
Erik Mosley and Derek Irvine, coauthors of The Power of Thanks

During the past several years, there has been a succession of "superheroes" presented to us on the silver screen, each one with more remarkable powers than the next. (*Iron Man* is one of my personal favorites). At the same time, in the real world, we have suffered through a seemingly endless series of embarrassing revelations about business, government, and community leaders who were once celebrated as real-life heroes.

This has prompted me to think a lot about those whom we celebrate in our organizations, wondering if we recognize the right heroes, or whether we inadvertently play into a cult of personality that can so quickly and easily develop around an organization's designated stars. How can empathetic leaders be sure to call out the examples that truly embody a company's values?

Feet of Clay

I recall a favorite high school English teacher (a dear and kindhearted nun, Sister Noreen) reminding us that "we all have feet of clay" (i.e., we may look very shiny and impressive on the surface, but under the surface, we all have the same human weaknesses and frailties). So true. To wit, in the span of a few recent years, we have come to learn that:

- A bicycle-racing champion, whose personal story of triumph over life-threatening illness inspired millions around the world, was ultimately stripped of his record-breaking titles due to admitted cheating
- A college football coach, whose name for decades was synonymous with integrity and leadership, was alleged to have looked the other way while a longtime aide repeatedly committed horrendous crimes against children on the very campus on which the coach held virtual god-like status
- The founder of what was once one of Silicon Valley's hottest tech startups fell quickly from grace when it was revealed that her company's technology was an alleged sham, resulting in criminal charges and potentially endangering the health of thousands who had relied on the company's medical testing results.
- The CEO of one of the world's largest auto manufacturers was arrested and stripped of his position for allegedly underreporting tens of millions of dollars in income.

So often, organizations create myths about their leaders and star performers that raise them to virtual rock star status of fame and fortune. They do this at their own peril, though, as when the fall from grace comes, it often occurs at a dizzying pace, leaving the individuals and the employees and fans who believed in them devastated and disillusioned.

Is there a better way to celebrate the day-to-day heroes who serve our customers and keep the ship of state running smoothly, often without recognition or acclaim?

Identifying Your Organization's Heroes

How can we identify and celebrate those who truly should be celebrated?

The first step is to define who we're looking for: the men and women who show up every day and do their jobs to the best of their abilities; the people who serve the customers, get the shipments out the door, and make the trains run on time. In short, these are the unsung heroes who make our companies what they are.

The next step is to seek them out. I've seen this done by:

- The CEO who, upon arriving at the manufacturing plant, bypasses the management wing of the building and walks straight onto the production floor to shake hands with the crew, to hear their stories, and to listen and respond to their questions and concerns
- The VP who sits side by side with her team on the floor every day instead of taking an office, taking in the day-to-day chatter and gaining first-hand insights into how things really get done in the department and in the company
- The operations leader who makes it a point to regularly visit all the company's locations, no matter how out of the way they might be, brings with him their favorite sandwiches or pizza, and swaps stories with the team over informal lunches and gab sessions.

By actively listening and engaging at all levels of the organization, it often becomes quickly apparent who the unsung heroes are.

Celebrating Them

The most impactful recognition, of course, is person-to-person; extending your hand and saying, "I know what you do for this company. I truly appreciate it, and I thank you." Beyond the one-to-one recognition, though, it is important also to publicly celebrate these individuals in some form so that others may see that these are the values and behaviors that you recognize and appreciate.

There is no limit to how they can be recognized. Possibilities run the gamut from awards to gift cards to special lunches, public ceremonies, etc., depending on what fits well with your culture. One of my personal favorites is to feature these individuals regularly in your employee newsletter or similar publication, as well as to put the spotlight on them in brief videos on your website's careers or values page, so that employees and potential job candidates alike can easily see the behaviors and traits that you value.

<u>AN EMPATHETIC APPROACH</u>

Everyone, even the most modest and unassuming among us, needs to feel valued and appreciated. By going out of our way to celebrate the unsung heroes in our organizations, we are sending a message without saying a word that we value and appreciate their efforts—and that makes all the difference in the world to the individual being recognized, and to the culture as a whole.

TIP #22:
LISTENING SAVES LAWSUITS

"Most people do not listen with the intent to understand;
they listen with the intent to reply."
Stephen R. Covey, The 7 Habits of Highly Effective People

"Too often we underestimate the power of a touch, a smile, a kind word, a
listening ear, an honest compliment, or the smallest act of caring, all of
which have the potential to turn a life around."
Leo Buscaglia, author

"Sometimes all a person wants is an empathetic ear; all he or she needs is to
talk it out. Just offering a listening ear and an understanding heart
for his or her suffering can be a big comfort."
Roy T. Bennett, author

Every time that I work with a manager to resolve an employee relations issue, I am reminded of the importance of *listening.* It's a simple notion --but taking people seriously by taking time to hear their story is not only validating for them on a personal level, it's also an important way to protect our organizations, as well as being a hallmark of a truly empathetic leader.

Hearing People Out and Taking Them Seriously

Many years ago, as a new HR person, I was put in charge of the organization's grievance process. Young and naïve, I dove into the task, listening intently to the grievants' stories (sometimes for hours at a stretch), and trying to help them through the process as best I could.

As background, it was very difficult to get fired from this nonprofit social service organization. Given that these individuals had already been fired (sometimes after years of warnings), the evidence wasn't often on their side, to say the least. In all of the cases I handled, each of the terminations were eventually upheld by an internal committee. However, none of the grievants pursued further action (i.e., no DOL or EEOC claims or lawsuits), even though it was their legal right.

In reflecting on this, a simple truth became clear to me: *People just want you to take them seriously.* Most didn't really have any expectation of being reinstated. They just wanted someone to hear their side of the story. Until that happened, they felt stifled and frustrated. Once they could tell their story, they could let it go more easily and move on to the next part of their lives.

Emotion and the Law

A wise employment attorney once shared his wisdom, saying:

"Employment law isn't about the *law*—it's about *emotion*."

Indeed. In the grievance cases, once we got the emotion out of the situation by hearing the individuals out, with attention and sincerity, everyone could move forward. It took some time and some patience (these weren't always the easiest individuals to interact with), but in the end, it paid off. The individual's dignity was upheld, and the organization achieved closure without cost.

AN EMPATHETIC APPROACH

It always pays for leaders to take seriously concerns from all members of their teams. You can't always do something to resolve their anxieties, but you can always listen actively and respond sincerely. Regardless of the circumstances, this always goes a very long way toward resolving the emotions of the matter for all concerned.

TIP #23:
READ THE MOMENT AND
ACT ACCORDINGLY

*"Do not dwell in the past, do not dream of the future,
concentrate the mind on the present moment."*
Buddha, philosopher

*"Hope is the magic carpet that transports us from the present moment
into the realm of infinite possibilities."*
H. Jackson Brown, Jr., author, Life's Little Instruction Book

*"For me, exploration is about that journey to the interior, into your own
heart. I'm always wondering, how will I act at my moment of truth? Will I
rise up and do what's right, even if every fiber of my being is telling me
otherwise?"*
Anne Bancroft, actress

It is good and necessary for an organization to have policies,
procedures, standards, and guidelines in order to function efficiently
over the long haul. Sometimes, though, it is the leader's job to sense
the uniqueness of circumstances and consider the broader
opportunities presented by that moment—and to leap into the abyss
and go for it. This is a story of one of those moments.

What Happened
One early summer evening not too many years ago, in an otherwise
forgettable season, at Citi Field, in the working-class borough of
Queens, in the City of New York, Johan Santana threw a no-hitter.
While a noteworthy accomplishment on its own (there have only
been 275 no-hitters in major league baseball since 1875), it is not why

grown men cried at the feat and an entire fandom was elated for days afterward. Santana's unique moment was set against the backdrop of many decades of prior heartbreak and shortfalls by his team, history which was crucial to his manager's brave action which is the crux of our story.

Backdrop

Santana was pitching for the New York Mets—a team nicknamed "The Amazins" not for their stellar play, but for their often-historic ineptitude, occasionally punctuated by fleeting periods of break-your-heart, so-near-and-yet-so-far brushes with greatness (cue the song, "Ya' Gotta Have Heart," from the classic musical, *Damn Yankees*, and you've got the picture). To wit:

- They came within one pitch of the World Series a few years prior, when they had the best team in baseball. That time, they lost in the bottom of the ninth of the seventh game of the playoffs with the bases loaded, a 3-2 count -- their best hitter at the plate, taking a called third strike that was perhaps the best pitch the opposing pitcher had ever thrown in his career.
- In the two seasons after that fateful strikeout, they suffered two of the greatest late-season collapses in baseball history, missing the playoffs both times on the last day of the season in almost inconceivably excruciating fashion.
- The collapses led to three losing seasons during which it was revealed that ownership had lost hundreds of millions of dollars in the Bernie Madoff scandal and otherwise couldn't seem to get anything right (e.g., dedicating the entrance to their new ballpark to a player from another team and somehow failing to honor great players from their own team's history).
- Seven Mets pitchers have gone on to pitch no-hitters for other teams after leaving the Mets. Most notably, despite

their fifty-year history of having outstanding pitchers, none had pitched a no-hitter with the Mets (one of only two teams with this distinction).

Thus, their no-hitter-less streak was 8,019 games and counting when Santana took the mound that fateful night.

Pitching for History

Before coming to the Mets, Santana had won two Cy Young Awards and was recognized as one of the best pitchers in baseball. In his first three seasons with the Mets, he pitched very well but suffered through considerable arm injuries. After intensive rehab, he (and his shoulder) seemed to have regained his old form that season. Then came that night.

Santana took the mound that night fully aware of the Mets' history, and knowing how much his performances encouraged an otherwise downtrodden fan base. He also knew how much his leadership on and off the field set the tone for his striving but overmatched teammates. "He sets the bar for us," pitcher Jon Niese said at the time. "Everybody feeds off him."

The Moment of Truth

When Santana got through the fifth inning without having allowed a hit, everyone watching knew something special might be brewing. They also knew that as he approached a hundred pitches (generally considered the safety limit for most pitchers these days), it would be virtually impossible for his manager to allow Santana to finish the game without seeming to risk the health of his surgically repaired shoulder. Then, in the sixth inning, when the Mets left-fielder virtually knocked himself unconscious crashing into the wall while making a catch to preserve the no-hitter, fans really started daring to hope that—pitch count or not—this might be "the night."

After the seventh inning, Mets manager Terry Collins approached his ace pitcher in the dugout. The safe money was on the manager following conventional wisdom and pulling Santana from the game to preserve his health. However, his mound ace stated in no uncertain terms his intent to finish the game. His manager didn't argue, and the die was cast.

Thirty minutes and two innings later, on his one-hundred and thirty-fourth and final pitch, the mission was complete. The Mets had a no-hitter. Santana was forever enshrined in New York baseball history. And a fan base, a team, and a culture so often short on hope had a moment of unadulterated joy.

AN EMPATHETIC APPROACH

It's only a game—except when it's not. Sometimes, at very special moments, it can be so much more. Just like it's always just business, except when it's not.

So, too, in business, empathetic leaders sense when special moments are at hand. At these times, rather than hiding behind "standard operating procedures" or being paralyzed by "corporate policy," they assess the moment and act with confidence to do what is needed, having the courage to take risks to act in the best interests of all involved.

Santana's manager, Terry Collins, read the moment and sensed that his player, his team, and his fan base wanted and needed the no-hit achievement that was finally in their grasp. He went all-in, and his confidence made it possible for his player to give everyone the moment that they were looking for. And it will be forever remembered, having a lasting impact on so many.

Post Script: It is a poignant footnote that Santana succumbed to injury again a few weeks later, and after a few additional rehab attempts, ended up retiring from baseball shortly thereafter. When interviewed years later, he still had a smile on his face reflecting on his achievement and his career. He blamed no one and stated he wouldn't have traded that special moment for anything – even a longer career. He did what he'd come to do in that moment, and he appreciated his manager for giving him the chance.

TIP #24:
CHANGE IS HARD (THE POWER
OF REPETITION)

"There is nothing more difficult to take in hand, more perilous to conduct, or more uncertain in its success, than to take the lead in the introduction of a new order of things."
Niccolo Machiavelli, The Prince

"Change is hard because people wear themselves out. And that's the second surprise about change: What looks like laziness is often exhaustion."
Chip Heath, Stanford Graduate School of Business

"It's the repetition of affirmations that leads to belief. And once that belief becomes a deep conviction, things begin to happen."
Muhammad Ali, boxer, international icon

I am often reminded how difficult change really is for all of us as employees, leaders, and human beings. For change to truly take hold in organizations, leaders must communicate why the change is taking place, *repeatedly*—and then act consistent with the change, *repeatedly*. Empathetic leaders remember that change is difficult for everyone and requires patience, fortitude, and consistent communication and action on their part.

Changing from a Top-Down to a Trust-Based Culture

As I was helping a group of front-line supervisors implement a new performance evaluation system, the question of trust kept coming up. Not quite getting it at first, I kept talking about how the system would free them to coach, mentor, and support their employees. And they kept asking, "Really?"

The system itself was simple, so I was confused, until it finally became clear that they weren't questioning the system, only their role in it. The "really" was, "Are you sure that the organization *really* wants us spending our time coaching and mentoring? They're *really* going to let us do that?" Clearly there was some emotional baggage to overcome before any new system could take hold.

The History

In the prior ten or so years, this team had experienced a succession of short-term leaders. With each new leader—some more trusting and empowering than others—the role of the front-line supervisor had shifted, leaving them confused and dispirited. The common theme, in the supervisors' perception, had been decisions got made at the top, without much explanation as to the whys and wherefores. They weren't sure what they were expected to do as managers, so they focused on their day job, serving customers with skill and joy, and tried to put aside questions of "what else" for another day.

The Breakthrough

To gain a deeper sense of the issues, I put a chart of cultural continuums on the board and asked the team to mark where they felt the organization's culture stood on each (e.g., individualist versus collaborative, judgmental versus supportive, etc.). When they made their individual marks and we stepped back as a group to view the results, we had our "aha" moment.

Most of the marks were on the left (negative) side of each continuum, speaking to an untrusting, autocratic culture. This was why they were having such a hard time believing that the new administration wanted them to coach and mentor their employees. Prior administrations had created such a long-running feeling of disempowerment and distrust that it was going to take the new team many months or years of consistent, supportive action before they would really believe that a change had occurred.

A Brief but Poignant Reminder of the Need for Repetition

In sales and marketing theory, they teach that a potential client must hear the same message as many as seven times or more before it begins to register and leads to action at any perceptible level. I was reminded of this again in a recent interaction with a senior leader who was a few months into his role attempting to turn around the culture and revenue of a company that had been experiencing negative morale amidst declining financial and operating results.

The leader, Devin, was an extremely bright, talented, and sincere leader. He sometimes struggled to remember, though, that not everyone assimilated information and understood and embraced necessary changes as quickly as he did.

As a case in point, early in Devin's tenure, an employee (Luke) in a remote office approached him, saying that it would help him be more connected to the team in the corporate office if he could visit the headquarters more regularly. Devin said, "I agree. Feel free to visit at least quarterly." In Devin's mind, the matter was settled, which was why he was frustrated when Luke made the same statement to him two months later, not yet having scheduled a trip to corporate.

When Devin shared his frustration with me, I tried to help him understand the background. I explained that the prior leader often talked about empowering employees but that, when push came to shove, employees were reprimanded for using their judgement and booking "unnecessary" trips, even when they offered strong business justifications.

Devin said, "Yes, I understand, but *I told* Luke he could make the trip."

"I know," I replied, "but that's exactly the thing. Luke has been so conditioned to getting his hand slapped for the using the smallest bit of discretion, he's going to need to hear your approval several more times before he even starts to believe that he is really empowered to make these decisions for himself now."

AN EMPATHETIC APPROACH

Empathetic leaders remember that people need to hear something multiple times ... and then see you reinforce it multiple times ... before they believe the change is real. Have patience. Stay consistent. Hang in there. They'll believe you—eventually.

TIP #25:
REMEMBER THAT "FIERCE CONVERSATIONS" REQUIRE RELATIONSHIPS FIRST

"There is something within us that responds deeply to people who level with us."
Susan Scott, Fierce Conversations

"Be candid with everyone."
Jack Welch, CEO, General Electric

"It's important to learn how to have conversations with other people where it's not debating but discussing. "
Karamo Brown, television personality

In recent years, there has been widespread interest in books recommending "fierce" or "difficult" conversations with "radical candor." While these best sellers offer many excellent communication tips, I worry that their most enthusiastic adherents sometimes disregard two vital prerequisites to success with these techniques; that is, establishing both the organizational culture and interpersonal relationships that must be in place prior to the conversations being launched. Without these foundations, the conversations become contentious and divisive rather than respectfully candid, productive, and forward-looking.

A Tale of Two Colleagues

James is fiercely bright, passionate about a wide range of subjects, and eager to engage in stimulating debate to help focus and fine-tune his ideas and perspectives. He feels morally compelled to question approaches to problems until rigorous, high-quality answers and results are achieved—all to the good.

Not surprisingly, James is a strong proponent of "fierce" conversations. Also not surprisingly, this can overwhelm those who don't share his same sensibilities. He has been known to open one-on-one meetings with the declaration, "We need to have a fierce conversation" which, while candid and sincere, often serves to immediately put the other party on the defensive.

When James was promoted to a formal leadership role, team members immediately respected his intelligence, commitment, and accomplishments, but quickly observed that his fierce approach made regular department meetings feel like daily public interrogations. In the end, the technical advances the department made under his leadership were arguably balanced out by the damage inflicted on morale from James' in-your- face communications style.

Anna is equally bright and shares the same thirst for excellence and passion for candid conversations as James. As with James, she has a remarkable ability to seek and hear constructive criticism and not take it personally. "It's always about the work," she is fond of saying. "It's not about me."

In contrast to someone such as James, though, Anna's temperament enables her to pursue candid conversations while remaining acutely aware of the emotional reaction of listeners and the state of her working relationship with them. Even while speaking directly, she communicates in her tone of voice, body language, and manner an underlying caring for the individual and a concern for maintaining the relationship. The result is excellent work, but without the collateral damage that unchecked fierceness could bring.

This has two important effects:

1. The people she interacts with feel respected rather than overpowered
2. The impact of the work is likely to be much longer lasting in both the people and organizations involved.

The Downside of Fierceness without Relationship

To use an example from a different organization, I once supported a senior leader, Damien, who was equally as brilliant as James and Anna, and who also shared their ability to seek and act on constructive criticism without taking it personally—a remarkable quality, indeed. He would often say to the leadership team and to the organization as a whole:

> "We need to speak to each other with fierce candor and with good spirit."

The difficulty that I often tried to share with Damien, though, was that he spoke with such intensity that listeners often saw and felt only the "fierce candor" style that he proposed, and they never heard the "with good spirit" part of his sentence.

I believe that the disconnect in this case was due to a lack of prerequisites (i.e., foundational understandings):

- **Unarticulated Values** – Damien was new to the organization and we hadn't yet agreed on or communicated our corporate values under his leadership. Thus, we didn't have a common understanding either of the intent or the boundaries around the ferocity of discussion that he favored
- **Assumed Positive Intent** – Damien's team hadn't worked with him long enough yet to be certain that he truly spoke with good spirit (i.e., respecting others, wishing them well, and working collegially for their success) when speaking passionately.

In cases such as Damien's, until the prerequisites are addressed and put into place by the organization, questions and concerns around the ferocity (and intent) of conversations will remain.

AN EMPATHETIC APPROACH

An empathetic leader understands that, in order for fierce conversations to be productive and culture-building, the prerequisites of defining and communicating the company's values, boundaries, and expectations in interpersonal communications need to be put into place. Once these are accomplished, the final piece is ensuring that all dialogue in the organization happens with the good spirit assumed above.

For this approach to work, it is critical that all members of the organization know and believe that:
- Their coworkers all have their best interests at heart
- Team members know how to share their thoughts openly and in a respectful way (e.g., disagreeing without being disagreeable)
- Everyone looks to support, improve, and encourage others -- and not personally demean, or degrade them.

Interacting in this way, in conversations small and large, formal and informal, day in and day out, builds credibility, which serves as the platform for constructive conversations. By doing so, conditions will have been set for conversations that can address important issues without being sabotaged by concerns about motives, hidden agendas, or harmful intentions. By establishing this foundation, "fierce" conversation become *constructive conversation* for mutual benefit.

TIP #26:
GIVE VOICE TO TRUTH-SAYERS

"Three things cannot be long hidden: the sun, the moon, and the truth."
Buddha, philosopher

"Face reality as it is ... not as you wish it to be."
Jack Welch, CEO, General Electric

The first duty of man is the seeking after and the investigation of truth.
Marcus Tullius Cicero, Ancient Roman statesman

"Never be afraid to raise your voice for honesty and truth and compassion against injustice and lying and greed. If people all over the world would do this, it would change the earth."
William Faulkner, author

Over the years, I've worked for several firms that have conducted annual employee surveys. As someone who believes deeply in soliciting, collecting, and engaging with all employee opinions, I'm always encouraged by the organizational opportunities for self-learning that these surveys represent. However, my experience is that the difficulty with employee surveys is in truly *listening* to—and then having the determination to *act on*—the results.

Empathetic leaders understand that most employees:
- care about the company and have many thoughts and suggestions that they want to share, if given the forum
- want to be taken seriously, and won't contribute meaningfully if they are skeptical that management either won't listen or is conducting the survey as window dressing

- don't expect management to act on every suggestion but need to see some action and forward movement in order to want to participate again the next time around.

To build and maintain the truly engaged employee culture that you are seeking, it is vital to not only act on survey results in a meaningful way, but also to seek out and encourage "truth-sayers" in all areas of the company throughout the year, not only at survey time.

Linus Speaks Up

One example of giving voice to truth-sayers is seen in the classic television special, *A Charlie Brown Christmas*. Towards the end of the program, ever-beleaguered Charlie Brown, despairing over the commercialization of Christmas (in 1965!), asks the central question: "Isn't there anyone who knows what Christmas is all about?"

His wise friend, Linus, steps forward calmly and confidently and gives an answer for the ages that gets right to the heart of the matter. (His answer—speaking his truth—is available on YouTube and elsewhere.)

It strikes me that Linus' answer, like so many organizational truths, was known to many but spoken only by a few. It took someone willing to ask the question, and someone willing to say what everyone was thinking, for the answer to come forth. In his despair, Charlie Brown inadvertently created the conditions by which the truth could come out: *he asked the question.*

Missing the Point

A company I'm familiar with used to conduct an annual employee survey. For several years running, the top-three answers to "What issues are holding us back?" were consistently:

- Communication between managers and employees is poor

- The company doesn't seem to have a clear direction
- I personally like my manager, but people don't have a lot of confidence in the management team in general.

Unfortunately, rather than trying to solve the communication and confidence issues that the employees identified, the management team—hurt and perplexed by the perennially negative results—decided to discontinue the survey. Opportunity lost, and wrong lesson learned (as well as being a classic case of blaming the messenger).

In contrast, companies that handle the employee survey process effectively take time for:

- **Reflection** – Thinking deeply about the results
- **Action** – Identifying the top three steps that they can realistically take to address concerns identified in the survey
- **Transparency** – Sharing survey results with all employees, and
- **Engagement** – Inviting employees to participate in developing and implementing solutions to address their concerns (as co-chairs, local project leaders, etc.)

It is often a several-month process, but when done well and with commitment from the top, can create an upward spiral of positive change that supports high engagement and morale over the long haul. And it all starts from asking the question(s) in the first place.

Giving Voice to Truth-Sayers

After a holiday party for a remote field office, I witnessed a senior leader engage with a truth-sayer in a remarkable way that spoke volumes about his commitment to hearing and encouraging sincerely-held criticism.

At the conclusion of a very nice holiday affair for employees and spouses in a cozy restaurant, several members of the local management team adjourned for a nightcap around the establishment's bar. As the senior leader joined the conversation, he noticed that one of the managers was discoursing passionately about some of the tensions between the local office and "corporate." While alcohol had loosened the manager's tongue somewhat, he remained very much under control and spoke with emotion, but not belligerence or indiscretion.

In some organizations, the senior leader might have shut down the speaker, quashing his views, or at the very least limiting them in his presence. This leader, though, took the opposite tack. Seeing that the manager was sharing his thoughts with good spirit (i.e., speaking out of sincere intention to help resolve an issue and make the company better), he engaged with him and asked him clarifying questions.

Satisfied with the man's intentions, the leader shook the manager's hand and encouraged him to continue speaking truth as he saw it— something that was surely circulated and commented on throughout the organization in the days afterward.

AN EMPATHETIC APPROACH

Empathy—identifying with the feelings of others—necessarily starts with trying to discern what it is others are feeling. This may be accomplished formally through annual or quarterly engagement surveys, for example, or by seeking out truth-sayers. In either case, seeking out and acting on the information gained not only forms a virtuous cycle of identifying and fixing issues, but it also cements the bonds of trust between a company and its employees.

Everyone wants to be heard, and everyone wants to be taken seriously. Asking for their thoughts, and taking them seriously, is the first step.

TIP #27:
IDENTIFY AND REVERSE
DOWNWARD SPIRALS

*"If we focus on the minuses, we go down the spiral. But if we are able
to focus on the pluses, we can become stronger and
put more meaning into our life."*
Petra Nemcova, fashion model

*"Fear stifles our thinking and actions. It creates indecisiveness that results in
stagnation. I have known talented people who procrastinate indefinitely
rather than risk failure. Lost opportunities cause erosion of confidence,
and the downward spiral begins."*
Charles Stanley, pastor

*"When you allow circumstances beyond your control to determine your
attitude and actions, you risk plunging into a downward spiral of hasty
decisions and faulty judgments, to overreacting, giving up too soon, and
missing those opportunities that always—always—appear just when you
think life will never get better."*
Nick Vujicic, Australian evangelist, motivational speaker

Even the best-trained and best-equipped organizations (see GE,
IBM, Microsoft, Apple, Sears, etc.) encounter rough seas from time
to time, sometimes of their own making. When suffering from self-
inflicted wounds that have damaged morale, it is critical for
leadership to recognize which of their actions or decisions
contributed to the negative atmosphere and to work to quickly to
restore hope and confidence before the bad feelings coalesce into a
downward spiral of despair.

The Symbolism of Annual Events

Several years ago, I observed a seemingly small decision that was actually quite damaging to morale and productivity at the time. This happened when an employer, after a very difficult year, canceled the company holiday party--an event in which employees in the company's main operating center placed great meaning, seeing it as deserved recognition and reward for their hard work and dedication. Morale, already weakened by a struggling economy and decreasing sales at the time, took a further dive when the cancelation was announced.

Happily, one of the most uplifting management decisions that I witnessed occurred the following year in the same organization, when the holiday party was reinstated. Management had sensed the negative morale that the prior year's cancelation had caused and reversed course, even though business had improved only marginally. They realized that it wasn't about the party itself; it was about the message that having or not having the party sent to employees as to how they were valued and appreciated (or not).

The energy and enthusiasm the employees poured into planning the reinstated party, and the resulting jolt to morale, more than paid for the modest costs of the event, and (along with a rising economy) set the stage for a dramatic upswing in business results the following year. Reinstating the holiday party sent the message that management appreciated the team's effort and believed that better days were ahead. The employees responded in ways that made this a powerful, positive self-fulfilling prophecy.

Other Reversals that Led to Renewals of Spirit

Other examples of this phenomenon include:

- **Punishment: No dinners allowed** – I observed a different organization suffer the same self-inflicted wound, only worse.

This time, a senior operations leader was angry at the management of a large facility and canceled their holiday party as "punishment." They were prohibited from having even a simple in-office employee luncheon while the company's other offices went ahead with catered, fancy evening affairs.

This was gravely damaging to employee and management morale in that location, ninety-nine percent of whom had nothing to do with the alleged transgression that had triggered the executive's pique. To his credit, the local manager, knowing the value of employee appreciation, discreetly gathered his team and their spouses for a quiet but heartfelt appreciation dinner at a local restaurant and paid for it out of his own pocket.

Happily, the next year, the company's new leader rapidly reversed the error and personally traveled to the location to host the holiday party (including spouses) in fine surroundings, with party gifts and mementos for all—topped off with the leader's talk highlighting his appreciation for their outstanding efforts overcoming significant obstacles throughout the year.

- **No Joy, No Basketball** – At another organization, one of the offices had converted unused warehouse space into a half-court basketball court for the employees to enjoy during breaks, lunch, and after-hours. It was a great way for a high-energy, competitive team to "blow off some steam" together, as well as a nice perk that gave the facility at least a partial Silicon Valley-like vibe.

Unfortunately, the head of the facility abruptly rescinded basketball privileges when she perceived that "too many" sales people were shooting hoops rather than working. She went so far as ordering the dismantling of the basketball hoop, laying it down on the court, where it remained for months as a haunting symbol of the bleak atmosphere that had enveloped the company as it worked through a daunting economic downturn in its primary line of business.

Happily, just as in the case above, new management came in shortly thereafter and immediately reassembled the hoop and encouraged employees to use the court. The explicit message sent by the new leader was: "I trust you to work hard, hit your goals, and have fun along the way. Now go do it." Whether coincidentally or causally (or a little of both), the location's profitability soared in the following months.

AN EMPATHETIC APPROACH

Empathetic leaders recognize the outsized impact that key symbolic acts such as holiday parties and valued perks have on employee morale, organizational culture, and ultimately, performance. No one likes when anything is taken away (in any aspect of life). Accordingly, it is best to think twice before rescinding even the most minor of perks.

When decisions are made that have inadvertent (but predictable) negative results, it is critical that the management team have the awareness and humility to recognize the cause and fix the errors as quickly and publicly as possible. The symbolism of a sincere "thank you" – whether in the form of a fine holiday dinner, a replaced basketball hoop, an after-work happy hour, or a simple, heart-felt word from the boss -- always far outweighs its cost in dollars.

TIP #28:
RECOGNIZE HOW EMPLOYEE FAMILIES SUPPORT YOUR CULTURE

"Take care of yourself: When you don't sleep, eat crap, don't exercise, and are living off adrenaline for too long, your performance suffers. Your decisions suffer. Your company suffers. Love those close to you: Failure of your company is not failure in life. Failure in your relationship is."
Ev Williams, co-founder of Medium and Twitter

"When you're gone, would you rather have your gravestone say, 'He never missed a meeting'? Or one that said, 'He was a great father.'"
Steve Blank, author of The Startup Owner's Manual

"That's one small step for (a) man, one giant leap for mankind."
Neil Armstrong, first man on the moon

In viewing *First Man*, the movie recounting Apollo 11 commander Neil Armstrong and crew's journey to the moon and back in 1969, I was reminded of the many burdens that our families carry for the sake of our work. As leaders, too often we downplay or diminish these burdens, when we should be recognizing and addressing them.

Empathetic leaders remember that the "whole person" comes into work each day, bringing with them the hopes and dreams, burdens and needs, and influences and passions of their spouses, children, parents, siblings and friends. In a very meaningful way, these influences and influencers (i.e., family members) need to be recognized, included, and cared for almost as members of your team.

Hopes, Fears, and Needs of Even the Bravest and Most Stoic

First Man provides not only a remarkable sense of what it was like to be in the historic capsule hurtling through space but is also an exceptionally moving and intimate portrayal of the many worries and stresses that the astronaut families bore, including the loneliness of lengthy separation, worry for the astronaut's extreme physical risk, and the resentment of spouses being left alone to tend to the family's needs. The script also illustrates the haunting effect that his young daughter's death had on Armstrong; a reminder of the unseen personal scars that we often carry into the workplace.

From a sheer physical safety perspective, family of military members, law enforcement, and first responders carry some of the gravest and most top-of-mind burdens: fear that their loved ones may not return to them each night. Countless other families bear the stresses of extended business travel, mandatory overtime hours, code sprints, hackathons, product launches, and the like that result in missed ballgames, dance recitals, and family events.

This is to say nothing of the disruptions of texts and emails on weekends or during vacations, and the fears, despite one's hard work and sacrifices, of potential layoffs, office closures, and relocations. In this way, our work can be more daunting to our families than to ourselves, as they have less control and influence over events than even we do.

Managers Who Get It

My uncle tells one of my favorite business stories about a time long ago (the early 1970s) when he was a young professional returning from his first international business trip for his well-known Fortune 500 employer. Upon his return, as he was preparing his first expense report, his manager took great pains to explain the company's (unwritten) expectation that he take his wife to dinner, treat his young daughter to a gift, etc., at the *company's expense*, in recognition of their sacrifices while he was away. I've always been struck by that story—a wise and empathetic manager, indeed.

In a similar fashion, I once served under a thoughtful leader who, shortly after coming onboard, insisted that the company reverse its long-standing "employee only" policy and start inviting spouses to holiday parties, along with inviting children and families to company get-togethers during the year. He knew that support from the family was vital and that recognizing and appreciating them was imperative.

This leader fervently believed that if the families got to know what the company was all about and interacted with leadership and co-worker families on a personal basis, it would create a bond that helped them support the employee's sacrifices for the company during difficult times. Indeed.

AN EMPATHETIC APPROACH

For all these reasons, as empathetic leaders, we are reminded of the need to show sincere appreciation and support for our employees' families, for their many unacknowledged sacrifices for the company's success. A little understanding, appreciation, and recognition goes a long way.

TIP #29:
KNOW WHEN TEAM-BUILDING ISN'T THE ISSUE

"Individual commitment to a group effort—that is what makes a team work, a company work, a society work, a civilization work."
Vince Lombardi, legendary football coach

"Teamwork is the ability to work together toward a common vision. The ability to direct individual accomplishments toward organizational objectives. It is the fuel that allows common people to attain uncommon results."
Andrew Carnegie, industrialist, philanthropist

Over the years, I have listened to a lot of sports talk radio. Invariably, when a local team is struggling, the hosts and callers will get into impassioned discussions about "team chemistry" and debate whether or not it adds up to wins and losses. The same question can be raised around team chemistry in business organizations: Does it matter if coworkers like each other? Respect each other? Enjoy working together? Does it make a difference to the bottom line, or move the needle in other aspects of the company (such as culture and employee morale)?

In my experience, when a management team is struggling, inevitably the suggestion arises that a team-building event is needed. Is this always the right prescription? It strikes me that team-building efforts, besides often being halfhearted or poorly conceived, are frequently premature (coming before, or instead of, resolving other, more deep-seated issues).

In assessing whether a team-building event is right for their organization at the time, empathetic leaders will strive to identify and understand the underlying issues, to ensure that any team-building events or interventions actually deal with the problem, rather than addressing mere symptoms.

Symptoms and Failed Prescriptions

A few examples from my experience:

- **Your Serve** – When a division's management team wasn't quite jelling, they decided they needed to spend more time together ... playing volleyball. The only problem was ... spending time together wasn't the problem. The fact that several members of the team weren't skilled managers and were individually failing in their roles (and thus weren't professionally respected by their peers) was the actual problem which no amount of bonding on a volleyball or badminton court, mini-golf course, or other venue was going to fix. Over time, as the underperforming members were eventually "counseled out" of the organization and replaced by more skilled managers, the division's performance (and that of the management team) took off.

- **We Need Another Retreat** – A leadership team that I was a part of was polarized. Good work was happening in the corporate office and in the field offices, but not necessarily in coordination (or cooperation). On more than one occasion, we tried to bridge the gap with a multi-day, off-site strategic planning retreat. We stayed at a nice resort, had lots of meetings (some led by expert outside facilitators), played some golf, enjoyed some delicious meals (steaks, cigars, cognac, the whole nine yards) ... and never quite came together.

The underlying issue: the corporate folks would say things like, "We think up the big ideas—we're the visionaries—and you guys (in 'the field') implement those ideas." (Having been one of the corporate people at the time, I cringe recalling that this was even thought, much less said out-loud, and imagining how it must have felt to the field team to hear it).

From the "field" people's perspective, they felt they were at least as experienced and capable as the corporate folks (they were), and they, understandably, were quite put off by being relegated to "just implementers." The problem wasn't just with the words; by all accounts, it seemed that the corporate group really thought they were smarter and more talented. No amount of gourmet meals or spa treatments was going to change that belief or bridge this divide.

- **Missing Common Values, Not Lunch** – In a small business I know, demand for products and services was high, and the management team was struggling to get a grip on managing internal operations. Their first initiative—changing the team's name from "Operations Team" to "Management Team" but without adding any authority for the team members over their departments—not surprisingly hadn't done the trick.

  Next, it was decided that the two team members who were struggling the most working together needed to go to lunch more often. After a few lunches, the idea was abandoned. In truth, the core issue was that these two individuals had very different business values and widely differing views of the meanings of excellence—a gap that a friendly lunch or two (or two hundred) wasn't going to fill.

Premature Prescription

Fair disclosure: As a general matter, I'm not fond of exercises like "try to build a perpetual motion machine using just these two twigs, some string, and a pencil" or other types of typical team-building ice-breakers or bonding activities. I'd much rather see candid, professional discussion of the actual issues at hand.

That being said, I'm not opposed to team-building events. I fully believe in the importance of getting teams to get together in a nice space, outside of the regular routine, and spending concentrated time getting to know each other better, working through important issues together. I just think that these events are often premature and end up trying to treat symptoms rather than the underlying "illness."

AN EMPATHETIC APPROACH

In each of the cases above, the underlying issue was that team members didn't respect or believe in the professional competence (and/or share the business values) of fellow team members. Where competence truly was in question, no amount of team building was going to make underperformers capable and respected by their peers. Until the team had the "right people on the bus," to borrow from Collins, the issue wasn't camaraderie; it was competence. Once that was dealt with, true team building could begin.

Empathetic leaders strive to identify underlying reasons for team-related struggles. They reflect upon what each member's wants and needs are that might be driving the immediate issue, as well as any pattern of issues. They try to get under the surface to ensure that any prescriptions are likely to address the underlying disease and cure it, not just ease the symptoms.

CHAPTER 4
LEADING BY EXAMPLE

*"As a leader, it's a major responsibility on your shoulders to practice
the behavior you want others to follow."*
Sue Bhatia, CEO, Rose International Group

"It's lonely at the top."
Anonymous

Empathetic leaders know that the ironic maxim, "Do as I say, not as
I do" simply doesn't work. As the leader, everyone's eyes are on
you—observing, assessing, interpreting, and making judgments about
your actions small and large. You must be prepared for this, and for
the pressure that comes with knowing that no one expects perfection,
but everyone expects authenticity. You must truly "walk the talk" if
you are going to gain and maintain the credibility and trust that is
vital to successful leadership.

While this chapter is all about your actions as a leader, the empathetic
leader understands that it is really all about the team, and how your
actions are understood, embraced, and followed by them. Tips
covered include:

* How symbolic actions signal how you want to lead and the
  messages you want to communicate

- Being resilient and genuine, and being sure you stick around until a problem is really fixed
- How you can shine a light on obstacles to help your team navigate safely around them
- Seeing self-discipline as a necessary trait and using it to powerful advantage in all that you do
- Knowing how to let go of team members who are hurting the team while maintaining the respect and dignity of all involved
- Demonstrating your positive, humble, and joy-filled spirit in all of your work
- Helping your team prepare for and adapt to change, so that they can progress to higher levels of achievement

TIP #30:
SET THE TONE WITH SYMBOLIC ACTS

"A good first impression can work wonders."
J. K. Rowling, author

"Almost everyone will make a good first impression,
but only a few will make a good lasting impression."
Sonya Parker, author

They say that you never get a second chance to make a first impression. This is why your first days and actions in a new role or company are so crucial in setting the tone for your leadership tenure. Empathetic leaders remember that everyone is watching their every move, however seemingly inconsequential, for clues as to your leadership style and priorities. It is important for your actions to be aligned with the messages you wish to convey.

Setting a Tone
As a Catholic, I recall being struck by Pope Francis's first moments on the world stage after being elected in 2013. Biographical reports on the previously unknown new pope remarked on his humble nature and penchant for avoiding the comforts attendant his prior role as bishop in his native Argentina. This nature was visible in his first actions as pope, standing on the loggia at St. Peter's Basilica in Rome before a television audience in the hundreds of millions.

- **Dress and Demeanor** – He elected to model simplicity by wearing a simple wood cross instead of an ornate, bejeweled one.
- **Names and Labels** – He chose the name *Francis*, modeled after St. Francis of Assisi, known for his commitment to the poor, to

symbolize his own outreach and connection to the poor and downtrodden.

- **Leadership Style** – Before he gave his first blessing, he humbly asked for the crowd's prayers and blessing on him, that he might be strengthened by those he would lead; servant leadership of the simplest but most powerful order.

- **Communication Style** – Pope Francis ended his brief talk by wishing the crowd a "good night and a good sleep" in the manner one would speak to an old friend or family member—setting the tone for how he planned to communicate with his worldwide congregation during his papacy.

A Picture (or Action) is Worth a Thousand Words

Throughout my career, I've observed several small but telling examples of leadership-through-symbolism that echo many of the symbolic actions described above.

- **Serving Drinks** – At our new CEO's first national management meeting, the team gathered at a local barbecue joint to get to know each other better in a relaxed setting. After quickly finishing his meal, the CEO got up and set about refilling everyone's glasses with lemonade, iced tea, or bottled beers. No one said a word, but everyone took notice that the leader was serving their needs.

- **Being Present** – Knowing his predecessor's reputation for distancing himself from the production floor, a new operations leader made it his business to greet each shift on his first plant visit with coffee and donuts—starting with the overnight shift that felt the most left out of the loop. Showing up at three a.m. and being present to the team said much more than any motivational talk could have done.

- **Expanding the Breakroom** – A new branch manager quickly learned that the remote location felt that their needs were often neglected or disregarded. To show that she heard them, the manager quickly arranged for expansion and upgrading of the breakroom (one of the team's longtime sore spots, knowing that corporate had fancy cappuccino and espresso makers and they couldn't even get approval for a simple Keurig machine at their location). She went further to get on her hands and knees (literally) and help with the laying of new carpet in the remodeled break room. From that moment on, the team was hers.

AN EMPATHETIC APPROACH

As human beings, we look for clues as to how our leaders think about us and care for us. If we keep this in mind, we can act in ways that are consistent with who we are as leaders, and which convey the messages that we wish to communicate (especially early on), such as inclusion, caring, service to others, courage, conviction, and camaraderie.

TIP #31:
STAY WITH A PROBLEM UNTIL IT'S RESOLVED

"You can't build a reputation on what you are going to do."
Henry Ford, American industrialist

"Happiness does not come from doing easy work but from the afterglow of satisfaction that comes after the achievement of a difficult task that demanded our best."
Theodore Isaac Rubin, American psychologist

In the immediate aftermath of Hurricane Sandy's massive destruction around New York City, Long Island, and New Jersey, many local leaders maintained an almost-constant presence on television, radio, and social media. It was instructive to observe that some who stood before the cameras disappeared from view quickly after the bright lights were off, while others stood in the trenches and solved important problems well after the last story was filed and the camera crews departed.

Truly empathetic leaders keep their constituents' (and employees') needs uppermost in mind and deed, until the job is truly complete.

The Approaching Storm

As Hurricane Sandy approached, leadership at the local, city, and state levels seemed to do a very good job getting the word out to the people. And then, when the storm hit even harder than expected, political leaders were everywhere to be seen—holding hourly press conferences, surveying the storm damage, and generally maintaining everyone's spirits with calm pronouncements, heartfelt compassion, and a palpable presence.

At the worst of times, political leaders rose to the challenge and showed their finest colors. It was inspiring to watch. Resources were marshaled, hope was spread, and there was a clear sense of direction, engagement, and by-your-side-every-step-of-the-way leadership.

And then a funny thing happened … as the days passed, and the TV spotlights started to dim, the politicians suddenly became harder and harder to find. This is natural, you might say: "Life goes on. We have to return to normal." Fair enough—except, the job wasn't done – not nearly. Tens of thousands of homes were still without power, their occupants waiting in the cold, stranded and forgotten without even an estimate of when they might be able to return to their homes.

As time wore on, gasoline lines persisted; rationing continued … but leaders who had proclaimed "we'll keep at it until every last light is turned back on" suddenly seemed passive and unengaged. Leaders who, days before, could move heaven and earth were now seemingly flummoxed (or perhaps just disinterested) by the details of reconstruction. The people suffered as many leaders became invisible.

The same thing happens in businesses as well, of course. I once was partnered with an executive on an acquisition who promised me that we would be blood brothers, standing side by side in battle, in getting the newly-acquired company integrated. Despite the fiery rhetoric … after our first planning meeting, I never heard from him again—ever!

Flying Under the Radar and Getting Things Done
In contrast to the above, there are the leaders who fly under the radar and just get things done. Many years ago, just as the internet was becoming a part of our daily lives, I was tasked with building a

company intranet. The only problem was, very few of the company's more than one hundred locations were online or had any way to connect to a central hub at that time. Without connectivity, an intranet site, no matter how well constructed, would be meaningless.

To my great relief and good fortune, I was able to find a mid-level IT director who believed in the project and promised to help. And he did so, in spades. Over the next year, he worked tirelessly behind the scenes, connecting locations one at a time or in small groups, whenever it was technically and fiscally possible. He kept me posted regularly along the way, as I was building the site's content. After a year, he had everyone connected, I had the site built, and we could launch.

As far as I know, no one in his chain of command said a word to him about his contribution, but I knew how vital a role he had played in getting the job done. I offered my personal thanks, of course. It was one occasion where the cliché that "We couldn't have done it without you" couldn't have been more true. He appreciated the remarks, and left it at that, content at knowing he made a difference. No big speeches or promises—just the hard work to get the job done.

AN EMPATHETIC APPROACH

When disaster strikes (in any form), it is important for leaders to be present and visible, offering information, plans, resources, and comfort. It is even more vital to stay with the problem (and the people) to conclusion, seeing to their needs.

Like the IT leader described above, plugging away until the job is done is the way leaders show that they truly have their employees' needs and interests at heart—and that they care enough to deliver.

TIP #32:
LIGHT THE WAY

"We are told to let our light shine, and if it does, we won't need to tell anybody it does. Lighthouses don't fire cannons to call attention to their shining—
they just shine."
Dwight L. Moody, *American clergyman*

"I can think of no other edifice constructed by man as altruistic as a lighthouse. They were built only to serve."
George Bernard Shaw, *playwright*

"If you are a lighthouse, you cannot hide yourself;
if you hide yourself, you cannot be a lighthouse!"
Mehmet Murat Ildan, *contemporary Turkish playwright*

All too often, hurricanes and other natural disasters lead to massive power failures, leaving millions seeking a light in the darkness. Photos and stories of devastated communities longing for relief bring to mind the image of a lighthouse as a beacon of light, hope, and safety. This is an apt metaphor for the role empathetic leaders can play in times of turmoil, addressing employees' fears and shining a light on the path toward comfort and safety.

Taking Accountability

During my time as a consultant, I had the occasion to help an organization run by experienced, dedicated, and charismatic leader, Ann. Ann was a longtime CEO who had a strong leadership team under her, and what seemed by all accounts to be a healthy and positive employee culture. Remarkably, though, she and her team felt that less than fifty percent of their employees:

- had a clear understanding of the organization's direction
- knew why the leadership team made the decisions they did
- and saw clearly where the organization was heading

—a circumstance that they attributed to poor communication on the part of management.

It struck me that this well-respected leader openly acknowledged she needed to do a better job of communicating the organization's vision and direction to her employees, taking full accountability, rather than dismissing her team's concerns and assuming that "everyone knows where we are headed." She was determined to redouble her communication efforts, which she believed would have measurable benefits to performance, productivity and morale.

Going Silent

In contrast to the commitment of Ann and her team to communicating better, faster, and more clearly, newer leaders that I worked with at different times would tend to go silent (without realizing it) in times of turmoil in the business. These young executives were each very bright, talented, and well-spoken. They cared deeply about their companies and poured their souls into helping the organizations succeed. Unfortunately, in each case, they hadn't yet learned to rely on their teams for support, nor had they learned to trust their employees' ability to handle the truth about the circumstances of the business.

When different forces caused revenues to take a steep dive, they would withdraw and allowed almost no one to help as they tried desperately to pull the company back toward profitability. In effect, they established "radio silence," while at the same time, their body language drew tighter and more tense by the day. As they worked late nights and weekends alone, the employees—seeing all of this transpire without hearing a word from leadership—assumed the worst, and morale plummeted. The situations weren't truly remedied until months later, when the young executives departed and new leaders were installed -- who promptly set about communicating as early and often as they could, to restore employee confidence.

Lighthouse Leadership

Empathetic leaders see the value in serving as lighthouses for their employees, offering:

- **Light** – shining forth, cutting through the fog of an uncertain environment
- **Hope** – giving confidence that the organization has a plan (or at least a direction) for the future, along with a path for getting there
- **Safety** – providing reassurance that someone is standing watch, guiding their ship toward safe harbor

<u>AN EMPATHETIC APPROACH</u>

In times of turmoil, employees need a leader who can speak clearly about the realities confronting them and lay out a path forward. Empathetic leaders sense their employees' concerns, address them openly, and in doing so, provide comfort and stability. This gives employees confidence that management is leading them toward brighter days, values them enough to tell them the truth, and trusts them to help participate in the company's recovery.

TIP #33:
SELF-DISCIPLINE IS THE CRUCIAL LEADERSHIP SKILL

"With self-discipline, all things are possible."
Theodore Roosevelt, 26th U.S. President

"The ability to discipline yourself to delay gratification in the short-term in order to enjoy greater rewards in the long-term is the indispensable prerequisite for success."
Maxwell Maltz, American surgeon and author

"Compassion, tolerance, forgiveness and a sense of self-discipline are qualities that help us lead our daily lives with a calm mind."
Dalai Lama

I had the good fortune to observe a longtime colleague handle delicate interpersonal issues with great skill time and time again. Over time, it struck me that each successful result was influenced as much by what he *didn't* do as much as by what he did. While seeming passive on the surface, the "not doing" took a great deal of active self-discipline.

Self-discipline is a vital yet under-appreciated leadership skill. Empathetic leaders must practice it at all times (a lofty goal, I realize)—understanding that any given moment is not about what is going to make us feel good, help us blow off steam, or assert our power or ego—but rather, it is about what our teams need from us in order to be successful. Self-discipline (such as listening more than speaking) is what helps us to begin to discern and address employee and organizational needs.

Don't Underestimate the Soft-Spoken, Unassuming People

Arthur is very low-key in nature—ever friendly, helpful, and hopeful. He is quietly supportive in an "I've got your back" way without ever having to say it because everyone knows it's true. While he doesn't have much formal power in his company, he does have significant influence with its rank and file, flowing largely from his personal qualities. Time and again, his self-discipline allows his authenticity (integrity, genuineness, and an unquestioned desire to act in the best interests of the organization and the individuals involved) to come through and carry the day.

The Mediation

By way of example, Artur was asked to informally mediate a long-simmering conflict between fellow managers—one (Chris) Type-A, high-performing but abrasive, the other (Pat), very bright but undisciplined and underperforming. Arthur served in his usual role as a sounding board and trusted go-between for all sides.

He undertook a series of separate candid conversations with Chris and Pat, bouncing back and forth between their offices in a manner reminiscent of a secretary of state's "shuttle diplomacy." In each conversation, he actively sought out and heard the concerns of the person before him and gently shared ideas of resolution. He was seen as an honest broker by all parties. Neither side cared that the other was also speaking with him because they had confidence that he would never share anything in an inappropriate or harmful way.

The "Not Doing" Part

Where did self-discipline come in? As I came to find out, Arthur actually had some very definite opinions about the parties and incidents involved. Yet, he never expressed an opinion to the parties, and never tried to influence the situation except in a way that was helpful to those involved. He was very careful and deliberate about sharing only as much "truth" as he perceived each was ready to hear at any given time.

In this way, he helped slowly but surely bring about a solution that all parties felt suited their needs.

While many would have been tempted to make a soapbox speech to advance their views during the many conversations, Arthur scrupulously avoided doing so. For all this, he received no credit for his role except for the tacit praise that comes from others seeking him out as mediator … and the thanks of this HR person, grateful to him for serving as a constant role model of professionalism and self-discipline over the course of the years.

Lessons Learned

Among the many lessons of self-discipline I learned from Arthur are:

- **Discretion is truly the better part of valor** – we can have as much (if not more) influence by what we *don't* say as what we do say
- **It's not about you; it's about them (and the greater good)**—i.e., in order to be an honest broker, self-interest and ego must be put aside to focus on the good of those involved.

Postscript

While I've known Arthur for many years, somehow I've only recently realized how self-disciplined he is in many areas of his life. An adherent of yoga and meditation (disciplining the mind, body, and spirit in alignment), he's also a very active "weekend warrior" athlete (training the muscles and the will, again). In fact, he trained intently for several months at a time and succeeded in scaling peaks on various continents when well past AARP eligibility age. I don't know how I missed the self-discipline on display all along!

AN EMPATHETIC APPROACH

From the standpoint of empathy, Arthur's self-discipline in thought and word avoided inadvertently clouding these situations with his own opinions and needs. His self-disciplined speech helped those who he was trying to counsel see that he was striving to understand their needs and desires, rather than focusing on his own—which is why they trusted and embraced his solutions. In this way, self-discipline led to credibility and trust ... and ultimately to resolution.

TIP #34:
BRING CLARITY WITH DECISIVENESS

*"It's a lack of clarity that creates chaos and frustration.
Those emotions are poison to any living goal."*
— *Steve Maraboli*, Life, the Truth, and Being Free

*"... it is precisely because the world appears to us to be multiple, ambiguous,
and paradoxical that we must strive to speak and write clearly."*
Mark Dintenfass, author

*"Indecisiveness is the number one reason for failure. Lack of ability to make
a decision in a timely manner causes most people to fail with their
projects and plans. Identify this challenge and decide to
no longer let it be a setback from your success."*
Farshad Asl, The "No Excuses" Mindset: A Life of Purpose, Passion, and Clarity

A number of years ago, National Football League (NFL)
commissioner Roger Goodell issued fines and suspensions related to
the "Bountygate" scandal that were unprecedented in league history
in terms of their severity and scope. Goodell's strong action in that
case reminded me of the clarity that the prudent, decisive use of
power can bring to an organization. Empathetic leaders understand
their employees' need for clarity and therefore strive for it in all
communications and actions.

Bountygate
At the time, news leaked that an NFL investigation revealed the New
Orleans Saints had offered cash bonuses ("bounties") for injuries
caused to opposing players. A week or so into the resulting media
storm, the commissioner announced suspensions and fines for the

Saints general manager, head coach, and defensive coordinator, costing them each millions of dollars and barring them from participating in part or all of the upcoming season.

When the news first came out, you could hear the proverbial pin drop in the pro-football world from the immediate shock. With this decision, there was no doubt who was in charge, whether Goodell was serious or not, and what was or was not acceptable in the league anymore. The commissioner had made it all very clear.

(Note: Longtime NFL observers will note that the commissioner has made several decisions in the years since Bountygate that are generally considered neither clear, decisive, nor well-considered—illustrating the difficulty any executive has in leading consistently over an extended period of time. The comments and reflections above focus solely on Goodell's Bountygate decision).

A Clear Decision Breaks a Long-Running Logjam

I observed something in my own organization that brought home a similar point about the power of clarity. Two well-respected, senior members of the firm had been at bitter loggerheads over a particular issue for many months. Seemingly endless debate and dialogue, both public and private, had resulted in a stalemate. The company president's hope had been for peaceful coexistence, without alienating either party. However, as the individuals' positions on the issue seemed to be mutually exclusive, conciliation hadn't brought peace but only deep frustration on the part of all concerned.

Finally, at the beginning of a subsequent team meeting, the president stepped forward and announced a decision—and the team had its moment of clarity. She spoke calmly and kindly, but decisively, leaving no doubt it was a final decision. With this, both parties could then move forward.

Until announcing her decision, the ambiguity of the situation had been holding everything back. Once there was a firm decision, there was clarity. And once there was clarity, both sides had an anchor whose position they could trust. With this anchor, adjustments (i.e., compromise) could be fashioned, and thus the peace was made—but only because a firm and final decision had been made.

Wisdom of a Corporate Veteran

A very wise person, a veteran observer of many a corporate battle, told me something about leadership long ago that I've never forgotten. "An executive might come in every day, put their feet up on the desk, and seem to relax for months on end," she said. "But there are going to be times—and it might be only once or twice a year—when the chips are down and we really need them. And if at those times they step up and make the right call, they're earning their pay and doing what we needed them to do." By removing uncertainty from ambiguous situations, leaders bring clarity, calm, and confidence to employees – qualities that are vitally needed in times of turmoil.

AN EMPATHETIC APPROACH

Empathetic leaders know that everyone wants a decisive leader. Everyone wants to know what the rules are, where they stand, and what is or is not acceptable. Being clear and decisive removes burdens and uncertainties from employees so that they can focus all of their energies on performing the tasks and responsibilities at hand, not wondering "what if this" and "what if that." With clarity can come progress.

TIP #35:
LEAD WITH GLADNESS, HUMILITY, AND HOPE

"They say a person needs just three things to be truly happy in this world: someone to love, something to do, and something to hope for."
Tom Bodett, author, radio host

"When you do things from your soul, you feel a river moving in you, a joy."
Rumi, 13th Century Persian poet

"Humility is not thinking less of yourself, it's thinking of yourself less."
C. S. Lewis, author

"Pride makes us artificial and humility makes us real."
Thomas Merton, Trappist monk, author, mystic

"Optimism is the faith that leads to achievement. Nothing can be done without hope and confidence."
Helen Keller

An empathetic leader understands that while there are many styles of effective leadership, employees are looking for a few simple but vital things from their leaders:

- **Care** – about their people and their needs
- **Confidence** – that today is going to be okay, and tomorrow is going to be ever better
- **Purpose** – the belief that they are part of, and working toward, something greater than themselves.

One way that impactful leaders communicate care, confidence, and purpose is exuding gladness, humility, and hope in their work. These traits are exemplified in two very different, larger-than-life leaders that I have followed for many years: Cardinal Timothy Dolan, Archbishop of New York, and filmmaker, vineyard owner, and entrepreneur, Francis Coppola.

The Servant Leader

One Christmas season not long ago, I had the pleasure of attending a Mass at St. Patrick's Cathedral in New York that was led by Cardinal Dolan. The Cardinal cuts a large presence, both in physical stature and personality. He's vibrant and gregarious, smiling broadly, constantly engaging his congregation, and more than holding his own against the backdrop of the grand gothic cathedral.

Observing him in this setting, several characteristics stood out:

- **Exuding Gladness** – Every aspect of Cardinal Dolan's body language virtually shouted, "I'm *so glad* to be *here* with *you*"— communicating his joy at what he was doing and his gladness in serving the people.
- **Humility** – Dolan carried himself in a way that said, "Forget about my title or position; at heart, I'm really the same guy that you watch the football game with over chicken wings and beer at the local sports bar."
- **Hopeful Expectation** – During his homily, Dolan related an anecdote about his dieting history. He told the congregation that he often gets discouraged quickly … and inevitably goes out for a juicy cheeseburger, fries, and a milkshake! Beyond the self-deprecating humor, the larger message was one of instilling hopefulness: "We're going to have our stumbles; it is part of life. Let's not lose heart and get down on ourselves; let's keep moving forward, toward our ultimate goals, with

hope and expectation, knowing that what we're doing is truly
our mission and purpose in life."

Inspiring Purpose, from Hollywood to the Vineyard

Francis Coppola has had a life and career worthy of a Hollywood
epic: coming from a first-generation immigrant family; scaling the
heights of the motion picture industry (directing *The Godfather* and
Apocalypse Now); achieving wealth and fame, followed by bankruptcy,
followed by winning it all back and then some; experiencing the
tragedy of losing a child; and ultimately going on to a remarkably
successful second act as the founder of a nationally-known winery,
and most recently, as a burgeoning eco-hotelier.

While there are many management and life lessons to be gleaned
from Coppola's ups and downs, one that resonates the most with me
comes from his experience making *Apocalypse Now* in the late 1970s.

At the time he launched his Vietnam war epic, Coppola was riding
high as one of a new generation of Hollywood princes, and it seemed
he could do no wrong. Suddenly, though, he ran into a remarkable
wave of obstacles: multiple *coups d'états* against the government of the
Philippines where he was filming, delaying production for months on
end; typhoons that destroyed his sets multiple times; lead actor
Martin Sheen's sudden heart attack; being so many millions of dollars
over budget that it risked leading his studio into bankruptcy; and to
top it all off, the fact that he hadn't completed the script when he
started shooting and wasn't even certain how he wanted the movie to
end.

In the end, he and his team all lived to tell the tale: Sheen recovered;
the film was completed; it won several Academy Awards, and later
went on to be voted number twenty-nine on the list of Top 100
Films of the Century. Accolades aside, the question for us is, how did
he do it and what can we learn from this?

I believe that Coppola succeeded by exuding gladness, humility, and hopeful expectation. To wit:

- **Gladness** – Every fiber of his being was devoted to the film. There was no mistaking the gladness and joy in his work, which he spread to all on the set and in the editing room.

- **Humility** – It may seem odd to ascribe the term "humble" to a Hollywood titan. While I'm certain that Coppola has as strong an ego as most others in his position, it takes a certain humility of spirit to say, in effect, "Look—I'm not sure if this is going to work. Heck, I'm not even sure how I want the story to end. But I truly believe that with us working together, we have the chance to make something very special and I appreciate the opportunity to try."

- **Hopeful Expectation** – Coppola was driven by his belief that he had something to say that could contribute to the national discourse in a country that was then reeling from the effects of Vietnam, Watergate, stagflation, and the general malaise of the late 1970s. Enlisting others in his cause, he brought them into a project that he believed could make an important impact on the country and the world. To harken back to the words of another icon of the times, John Lennon, it's as if Coppola was inviting them to "Imagine" the possibilities of the world that they could create together.

AN EMPATHETIC APPROACH

Empathetic leaders understand that all teams and individuals look for leadership. Even the strongest individual contributor seeks the comfort of knowing that a leader they have confidence in is at the helm, steering the ship and its inhabitants through calm seas as well as turbulent ones, pointing toward the best days that are yet to come. Empathetic leaders can create this confidence and comfort among their teams by exuding gladness, humility, and hopefulness in their daily work which will capture their team's hearts and minds, and move them forward together.

.

TIP #36:
Help Your Team Graduate to New Levels of Success

"My wish for you is that this life becomes all that you want it to.
Your dreams stay big, your worries stay small, and that you
never need to carry more than you can hold."
Rascal Flatts, "My Wish for You"

"Wherever you go, go with all your heart."
Confucius, philosopher

"Go confidently in the direction of your dreams.
Live the life you have imagined."
Henry David Thoreau, American poet

"Do all the other things, the ambitious things—travel, get rich, get famous,
innovate, lead, fall in love, make and lose fortunes ... but as you do, to the
extent that you can, err in the direction of kindness."
George Saunders, American writer

Several years ago, I was responsible for managing the HR side of mergers and acquisitions for our division, which was a major part of our growth strategy. In one acquisition, we were purchasing a small fifty-employee private company in Denver, in a new, complementary line of business.

Because everyone was being retained after acquisition, it was a smooth and pleasant experience working with the owner, Sherry, on transition plans leading-up to the employee announcement. It was how this gifted leader handled communicating the acquisition to her employees that stands out in my memory as a shining example of empathetic leadership.

Taking Cues from The Owner

During any acquisition, employees take significant cues from the owner as to whether or not to embrace the acquiring company. If the owner demonstrates seller's remorse even before the sale is finalized, out of loyalty to the owner, employees will often feel compelled to resist the acquiring company's policies, benefits, and overall way of doing business. If, however, the owner communicates that the acquiring company are "good people" and that she's confident that her employees will be well-cared for, the path toward maintaining employee engagement and morale is greatly eased—which is exactly what happened in this case. I've never seen the handoff done so well as Sherry did it.

Champagne and Cookies

The day before the acquisition was going to be announced publicly, Sherry called a meeting of her troops. Amidst streamers, champagne, and cookies befitting a graduation party, she toasted her employees, saying, "I'm so proud of the work we've done together these many years, and I so deeply appreciate and value each and every one of you and the contributions that you've made to our success. As a small token of my appreciation, I have a gift for each of you." At that point, she handed out envelopes with bonus checks based on each employee's length of service. All were significant, with many extending into the tens of thousands of dollars, and all came from her personal proceeds.

"Not the Same"

After the rejoicing and tears, she continued, "I know that many of you are concerned about my selling the company. 'It's not going to be the same,' and 'We don't know that company—how do we know that they'll treat us right, or even keep us around?' are some of the questions I've been hearing in the past few days.

You're right—it's not going to be the same . . . I really do believe that it's going to be *better*. Here's how I see it:

"You've done terrific work and helped us get as far as we have. But we have our limitations as a small firm, and I wanted to see us progress even further. Now, with the new company coming in, the sky's the limit. Please don't feel that it is the death of the old company but rather, you've worked so hard, and now you've earned your graduation to the new company in the same way that your hard work in high school entitled you to graduate and move on to the even bigger and better things that college held in store for you. So, I thank you from the bottom of my heart . . . and I wish you, 'Happy Graduation.'"

And with that, among more champagne, cookies, and embraces, she presented each employee with a graduation scroll, symbolizing both her words and their transition to the next phase as an organization.

Setting Up for Success

To no one's surprise, with that sendoff, the office transitioned into our company as smoothly as any of the dozens of acquisitions we conducted during that period and soon was one of the highest-performing units in the division. Of course, this wasn't solely due to the former owner's graduation toast, but that toast was indicative of a mindset that created the positive environment for change, enabling quick success in their new world.

AN EMPATHETIC APPROACH

How Sherry handled the transition to the acquiring company is virtually the definition of empathetic leadership.

- She considered how her many longtime employees would feel and react upon hearing the news, and she planned the announcement to ease their minds to the greatest extent possible.
- She also knew that—as happy for her and her (perceived) windfall as they might be—even the most selfless among them would be silently wondering, "So, what do I get for all of my years of hard work and commitment?" She answered this with the unexpected personal bonuses.
- Finally, she knew that her team would take their cues from her as to how much they should trust and embrace the new company.

By handling their "graduation" the way she did, she set them up for success in the new company in the best way possible.

CHAPTER 5
COACHING AND
MENTORING

"Tell me and I forget, teach me and I may remember,
involve me and I learn."
Benjamin Franklin, American statesman, inventor

mentor (n.)
1. a wise and trusted counselor or teacher.
2. an influential senior sponsor or supporter.
-- synonym: adviser, master, guide

guide (v.)
3. to accompany (a person or sightseer) to show points of interest and to
explain their meaning or significance
Source: dictionary.com

Taken together, the quotations above describe my experience with
those that I have considered mentors, even if we never said the word
mentor out loud. As with many things in life, these individuals don't
necessarily fit a particular mold, other than that they offer their
kindness to those who come across their path.

Advice shared in this chapter's tips and anecdotes includes:

- Working hard to thoughtfully prepare all stakeholders for proposed changes
- Developing your team members so that they can spread their wings in new and exciting directions
- Supporting and encouraging young managers with your counsel and guidance
- Recognizing that mentors come in all varieties and vocations, and that they share their wisdom with us by providing examples in action
- Eagerly sharing your knowledge and experience with your protégés and mentees and focusing on their needs.

TIP #37:
PREPARE THE GROUND FOR SUCCESS

"Do your planning and prepare your fields before building your house."
Proverbs 24:27

"Preparedness is better than hope."
Alexis Romanoff, Russian admiral

"By failing to prepare, you are preparing to fail."
Benjamin Franklin, American statesman, inventor

*"Give me six hours to chop down a tree and I will spend
the first four sharpening the axe."*
Abraham Lincoln, 16th U.S. President

I once had a front-row seat to a business saga that, unfortunately, I knew wouldn't end well. Sam, a business development director, was preparing to propose an exciting new partnership to his company's executive team. If accepted, it could transform a significant aspect of the company and further enhance its industry-leading position. Unfortunately, it became clear early on that Sam's proposal was likely to be rejected out of hand because, as groundbreaking as his concept was, he failed to prepare the ground socially, emotionally, and "politically," so that the project might be accepted.

The Good, the Bad, and the Ugly

Sam's idea represented the culmination of years of work to understand and serve the needs of his customers. The success of this particular venture would depend heavily on a partnership with another organization. However, the leadership of Sam's company had a very negative history with partnerships stretching back decades—

including a recent disappointment with an underperforming partnership that Sam had also brought them not long before. Compounding matters, Sam had a very contentious relationship with Maury, one of the executives responsible for deciding the project's fate. This proposal, if implemented, would require close, ongoing coordination between Sam and Maury.

Moving Forward Before Bringing Others Along

Sam was deeply committed to his organization and his clients but he was generally prone to putting the cart before the horse, leaping forward with enthusiasm before assessing whether the ground was stable enough to support his success. In this particular case, his blind spots were:

- **Not getting out ahead of objections** – Sam had talked with the executive team as his concept developed from a "rah-rah" perspective, rather than an "I know you have concerns—how can I help address them?" framework. He felt that the obvious (to him) merits of the project should outweigh any of the executives' personal trepidations.
- **Relying on flowery speech over preparation** – Sam was a charismatic speaker, and his considerable rhetorical gifts made it easy for him to win over many an audience. However, in this case, it was unlikely that even the most inspiring talk could, by itself, overcome such negative history without considerable advance ground preparation to increase management's comfort with the proposal.
- **Choosing animosity over collaboration** – Sam's antipathy toward Maury led him to avoid building any relationship bridges in advance of submitting the proposal. He couldn't bring himself to approach Maury and say, "This project is too important for us to let personal feelings get in the way. It can be a great thing for everyone involved. Can we work together

for the good of the company and the clients?"

In the end, the executive team was intrigued by Sam's proposal, but, unsurprisingly, they decided against implementing it. Sam was crushed and went into a weeks-long funk as a result.

In candid discussion afterward, Sam acknowledged several blind spots that kept him from taking steps that would have made approval of the proposal more likely. It is unfortunate that Sam didn't have a manager or mentor who he had a close, trusting relationship with, who could have coached him through the process when success was still possible.

AN EMPATHETIC APPROACH
An empathetic leader anticipates where their mentees may have weaknesses or blind spots that may be preventing their success, and they are able to patiently counsel putting aside pride to do the work necessary to prepare for success. Without such guidance, much otherwise good work may be for naught; with it, a bountiful crop may grow and flourish.

TIP #38:
LEAD BY TEACHING (LESSONS FROM THE DELI GUY)

"A teacher affects eternity; he can never tell where his influence stops."
Henry Adams, American historian

"The dream begins, most of the time, with a teacher who believes in you."
Dan Rather, news anchor

"The greatest good you can do for another is not just to share your riches but to reveal to him his own."
Benjamin Disraeli, British statesman

"How to prepare someone for leadership:
I do it.
I do it and you watch.
You do it and I watch.
You do it.
You do it and someone else watches."
John C. Maxwell, management expert

I'd like to share with you a story about my deli guy. Because, in addition to making great sandwiches ("I'll take a 'Gerty'—corned beef and pastrami on rye with Russian dressing and a side of coleslaw. Thanks!"), he's also one of the most natural teachers that I've ever observed, and therein lies the story.

Dad's Deli and Training Academy
Dan, a longtime restauranteur and caterer, comanages Dad's Deli with his spouse and partner, Donna. Located in a modest building in a suburban setting, Dad's has developed a loyal following.

Beyond the quality of the sandwiches, this is due in no small part to the friendly, everyone-knows-your-name atmosphere (think *Cheers* in a deli) that starts with Dan's greeting as you enter the door.

A natural networker, Dan goes out of his way, even in the busiest rush periods, to make a connection with everyone who walks in. He'll remember your name, where you went to school, that you have a child in youth lacrosse or on the traveling soccer team, etc., and odds are he has some connection he'd be happy to introduce you to who can help you in something you're doing.

Guiding and Instructing

There's one other thing Dan is a natural at, and that is teaching. In fact, it's how he runs his business. Picture a busy Saturday morning: customers coming in eager for ham-and-egg-on-a-kaiser sandwiches, OJ, and coffee, while at the same time, the crew is gearing up to get trays of sandwiches, salads, and hot entrees loaded into trucks for delivery to that day's catering clients. Dan presides from in front of the grill, directing traffic, keeping a keen eye on quality control—and always instructing.

Whether it is showing a young assistant how to arrange a tray of sandwiches or cook eggs for six different orders at the same time, with every instruction, he's reinforcing "here's how to do it" with calm encouragement. That's not to say that his guidance isn't occasionally met with a rolling of the eyes or an "*I know*, Dan, I know" from his more experienced staff. The intent, though, of guidance and support is always felt (even in the moments of exasperation).

There's one other thing that Dan-the-leader does, and that is seeking out growth opportunities for his crew. For example, opening on Sunday may or may not be profitable for Dan, but when his eager young clerk asked for the chance to step up and run his own shop one day a week, Dan readily agreed. For this, he is repaid with the loyalty of his team, and the satisfaction of knowing that he is making a difference in the lives and careers of those he comes in contact with.

AN EMPATHETIC APPROACH

A recent MetLife study of benefits and workplace issues found loyalty to *company* being steadily replaced by loyalty to *individuals*. If one's manager is the embodiment of the company for most employees, what would it do to employee loyalty and engagement if all our frontline supervisors managed like Dan manages—leading by teaching? By looking out for the needs of their employees and customers—and always teaching, mentoring, and connecting— managers like Dan embody the best qualities of empathetic leadership. "Sandwiches on the house, all around!"

TIP #39:
HELP YOUNG MANAGERS GAIN THEIR FOOTING

"The challenge of leadership is to be strong, but not rude; be kind, but not weak; be bold, but not bully; be thoughtful, but not lazy; be humble, but not timid; be proud, but not arrogant; have humor, but without folly."
Jim Rohn, entrepreneur, author, and motivational speaker

"To handle yourself, use your head; to handle others, use your heart."
Eleanor Roosevelt, U.S. First Lady

"Fit no stereotypes. Don't chase the latest management fads. The situation dictates which approach best accomplishes the team's mission."
Colin Powell, U.S. General, Secretary of State

During my career, I've often had the pleasure of watching new managers grow into their jobs. It's always a treat to watch someone embrace a new role or endeavor with their whole heart, and to watch them progress as they master skills, gain perspectives, and find their own voice and style. As with any coaching endeavor, I've learned more from them during our formal and informal coaching discussions than I'm sure I've imparted in wisdom or insight.

A central theme of empathetic leadership is understanding situations from the other person's perspective. To that end, the following are a few observations where I've seen young managers both thrive and struggle as they wrap their minds around their new role guiding others.

Qualities That Help Them Succeed

- **Eagerly studying their new craft** -- My young friends approach management as a skill to be learned, and they dive into it with passion. They try to read and think about management skills and techniques wherever and whenever they can. Sometimes the mind gets ahead of the body, as it were (i.e., their desire to learn outpaces their actual skill at using the techniques they are learning) … which inevitably brings hard-earned experience and, ultimately, greater skill.
- **Empathizing with their team** -- Since they were only recently on the other side of the table, they are generally very good at empathizing with the needs, feelings, and perspectives of their team members. Recalling how they felt in prior positions when they weren't supported or encouraged, they conscientiously strive to provide their teams with the resources, backing, and autonomy they need to do their jobs.
- **Learning from veterans** -- Almost intuitively, my young friends have set about finding mentors and picking their brains on managing teams, handling interpersonal issues, etc. The veteran mentors benefit from this sharing, too, in all the ways that any teacher benefits from sharing knowledge with any student—and a virtuous cycle of learning, growth, and a trusting bond is set in motion.

Where They Often Struggle

- **Not being able to easily move from "bud to boss"** -- The downside of being able to empathize with their team is that it is often difficult to move from peer to supervisor without inflicting some damage on prior personal relationships in the workplace.

As peers, they were often friends outside of work with many of those they are now charged with evaluating and giving assignments, raises, and sometimes corrective action. It takes a mature individual to understand that the work part of their relationships with their team is now different and that they are no longer "one of the gang" in the same way as before.

- **Learning to delegate**
  Delegation might be the hardest skill to learn for most new managers who have generally been promoted due their technical excellence in their field, not their managerial skill. They begin to understand that their job is now to get work done *through* other people, rather than operating as an individual contributor.

  Under pressure, though, they tend to slip back into "I know how to code, and I'm better than Bob, anyway, so let me just take care of this for him and save us both the headache" mode—and need a gentle reminder that they are now more delegator than "doer."

- **Learning to balance the short-term with the long-term**
  The young managers often struggle to balance the allure of immediate gratification (i.e., results *today*) with the need to build the team's capacity (i.e., results in the *future*). Slowly, they start to understand that by taking time to fill Sally in on the big picture regarding "Project X" now (even though they don't really have the time, and she only has a small piece of the project anyway), they are setting her up to make a bigger contribution in the future, a contribution that might not be possible if she was only given instruction on her very limited task today.

AN EMPATHETIC APPROACH
Except for those in Fortune 500 or other well-established

organizations, my young manager friends commonly seem to lack much formal guidance from their immediate leaders (who themselves wear many hats and often don't see mentoring as part of their job description). By taking the time to talk with young managers about what they're seeing, feeling, learning, and doing—whether formally or informally—an empathetic leader is investing in both the young manager and the company's future. No matter the short-term results, this is always a wise investment of time and effort.

TIP #40:
MENTOR WITHOUT USING WORDS

The author's grandfather in his shoe repair shop, circa 1986

"Preach the gospel always. Use words when necessary."
St. Francis of Assisi

"The greatest good you can do for another is not just to share your riches but to reveal to him his own."
Benjamin Disraeli, British statesman

"Teach them the quiet words of kindness, to live beyond themselves. Urge them toward excellence, drive them toward gentleness, pull them deep into yourself, pull them upward toward manhood, but softly like an angel arranging clouds. Let your spirit move through them softly."
Pat Conroy, The Prince of Tides

A chance encounter with a friendly shoemaker in New York City got me to thinking about the personal values we bring to work. This gentleman who, to my amazement, stopped what he was doing as I entered his small shop and offered to fix my shoe while I waited (I didn't know that anyone did that anymore!) When he then proceeded to do so with great care and expertise, it reminded me of my late grandfather, a longtime shoemaker himself. In truth, this encounter and the response it provoked in me had nothing to do, really, with shoe repair and everything to do with the idea of mentoring through service, without saying a word.

Leather Dust, Opera, and Lunchtime Life Lessons

My grandfather began his career as a shoemaker as a nine-year old boy in Sicily. He emigrated to the U.S. in the 1920s, opening his own shoe repair shop in Elmhurst, Queens, a few decades later. He was a kind, proud, hard-working, happy man with strong hands, and fingers blackened by seventy-five years of working with leather.

He enjoyed his work and put his heart into fixing his customers' shoes to "as good as new" every time. But leather soles, heels, and taps weren't the only things on offer in his shop or even the main reason many of his regular customers came by the shop. With Italian operatic music or lush ballads in the background, he was always eager to share a story, ponder a bit of philosophy, or inquire about your family in heavily accented English accompanied by a warm smile.

As I came to understand as I grew older, while shoemaking was his profession, helping people—with a word of support, a twinkle in the eye, or a hand of friendship—was his vocation, and he practiced it every day, day after day, year after year, well into his eighties, in that little shop in Queens.

Sharing Your Values

It was that vocation of using his work to help people in ways large and small that he passed down to my father, who passed it down to me. Though the context has changed—from a shoe repair shop, to a social service office, to an HR department— the purpose hasn't changed: *Do what you can to help someone. Every day.*

For my father, that meant working around a cold and unsympathetic bureaucracy to find ways to aid those in need. For yours truly, it means trying to help companies attract, develop, and support people to fulfill the organization's mission (and their own). It is all about helping people and groups move forward, little by little, day by day.

Mentoring Without Words

It is noble and necessary to help others, of course, but how, exactly, was my grandfather a mentor? Well, if mentoring is all about exposing others to the many beautiful things in the world, and helping them see their place in it, and supporting and guiding them as they explore how they can learn to share their gifts with others, then this describes my grandfather's work exactly. It played out as:

- Exposing his visitors to the love of music in the joyful notes of the operatic tenors and lush symphonies, as well as the smooth voices of the Italian crooners of the time
- Chatting with his young children and their friends as they stopped by during their lunch period; hearing their daily hopes and struggles, and advising them along the way
- Greeting all with friendship and warmth; demonstrating how to embrace, support, and encourage friend and stranger alike.

Translation for Business Leaders

While these fond anecdotes are far removed from corporate or organizational settings, I believe that they still bear lessons in empathetic leadership. To wit:

- **Sharing with others your joy in your chosen field** – be it coding, engineering, the creative arts, or management and inspiring them to take up the further study of fields that light their own professional and personal passions

- **Exposing them to new and unknown ideas, cultures, and arts** – helping them see all that is possible in the world, and the many paths of exploration that they may take, both within your organization and outside

- **Hearing their concerns and giving gentle, heartfelt guidance from your own experience** – By taking seriously the concerns of his children and their friends, my grandfather gave them confidence that their community cared for them and would be there to help point the way in good times and in bad. In the same way, wise leaders provide reassurance and a kind and mentoring ear for their young charges when they stumble or struggle.

I realize that, to some, this may seem far afield from managing a business, but really, it is not. As leaders, we all have as our job-sharing passion for our field, exposing team members to all that is available to them, and hearing their concerns and sharing guidance and wisdom. These things we can do every day.

AN EMPATHETIC APPROACH

For his lifelong support of his local community of immigrants, my grandfather was given the designation of "Cavaliere" signifying, literally, a cavalry officer who leads and serves his troops. By understanding that your team seeks guidance, safe exposure, and caring direction as they explore the world around them, an empathetic leader can lead as a cavaliere does, pointing the way without saying a word.

TIP #41:
MENTOR THROUGH OTHERS

"You meet a new person, you go with him, and suddenly you get a whole new city ... you go down new streets, you see houses you never saw before, pass places you didn't even know were there. Everything changes."
Samuel R. Delany, author, Dhalgren

"The world unwraps itself to you, again and again, as soon as you are ready to see it anew."
— Gregory Maguire, playwright, Wicked

"The best way a mentor can prepare another leader is to expose him or her to other great people."
John C. Maxwell, management expert, author

"A candle loses no strength by sharing its light with others."
Unknown

Often, we're prone to think of mentoring as serious conversations in formal settings, where the veteran imparts wisdom to their protégé in one-on-one discussion. While that's one way that mentoring occurs, it's not the only way. Other mentoring happens just by thoughtfully and actively exposing someone to new ideas and experiences and others who can help them learn and grow.

As with all empathetic leadership, it is all about understanding and addressing your mentee's needs. When mentoring through others, you can bring things full-circle by discussing with your mentees their new experiences, helping them put these ideas and explorations in context, allowing you both to take in the journey together.
I'll discuss two such experiences here.

Introducing Them to a Whole New World

Attending the annual Society for Human Resources Management (SHRM) conference a few years ago got me—in the words of one of the main speakers—"geeked." (I hadn't heard that expression before but he's a super-enthusiastic guy, so I'm pretty sure it's a good thing). My geeking wasn't because of the keynote speakers or the other presenters (who were all very engaging, sharing useful nuggets from their personal stories about helping organizations develop). Those were nice benefits, of course. However, the greater benefit for me was being able to take a junior member of our team and share the experience with her as she began to see her professional world in a whole new light and on a whole new scale.

Six months before, I had registered myself and our junior recruiter, Sarah, for the conference, not knowing exactly where she would be in her growth curve when the date arrived. Nevertheless, I had a strong conviction that exposure to fifteen thousand fellow professionals would be a valuable learning experience by itself, regardless of whatever particular workshops would be offered. While I tried to impart tips and tidbits to Sarah (who reported to me) on a daily basis, I was limited, of course, by my own knowledge and experience— which pales in comparison to the collective wisdom of fifteen thousand high-energy, generous, sharing HR professionals.

Being only a year or two into her career, I wanted Sarah to see and feel what her profession is all about, to have her hear new (and often conflicting) ideas, and to know people's stories of overcoming adversity on their way to becoming leading professionals ... the same growth path that she's on. In the near-term, she emerged from the conference with a few new ideas that she set about putting into practice right away. Most importantly, though, the experience started to shape how she thought about her profession and her potential path. In that way, I'm very grateful for the help of fifteen thousand new friends and colleagues in shaping and guiding that path for

Sarah.

Gaining Skill Through Hands-On Exposure

On multiple occasions, I've seen a senior leader mentor young protegees to grow so significantly that they ultimately assumed top leadership spots – all through the benefits of intentional exposure. In these cases, the senior leader would purposefully hire a junior executive as their right-hand person and protégé. When the pair clicked, the senior leader would quickly begin entrusting their young charge with newer and broader assignments that stretched their skills and experience further and further.

The protégées immersed themselves in these projects and soon found themselves traveling widely, making new contacts across industries, and learning deeply all the key areas of business operations – from sales and marketing, to systems and data security, and everything in-between. In addition to personally mentoring the protégées in business topics in which they were highly skilled, the senior leaders would also purposefully set up the protégées to learn from other experts in areas in which they weren't nearly as knowledgeable. They learned quickly and were soon on paths to assume the most senior roles.

Learning from the Good and the Bad

By being exposed to an ever-expanding range of new projects and functions, the protégées wer able to develop skills and knowledge much more rapidly and deeply than they would have if they had been limited to smaller projects or had not had the freedom to pursue projects where they might lead, regardless of short-term costs or resources (within reason).

The unfortunate (and deeply ironic) downside of these senior leader-protégé relationships is that – for whatever reason – it was commonly observed that the protégé-turned-leader often didn't heed the lessons of their own career growth when they assumed senior roles. Sadly, they often appeared reluctant to give junior members of their own teams the same type of broad, impactful assignments that would have served to build up their skills, just as their mentors' stretch assignments had helped them when they were the young protégées rapidly working themselves up the ranks.

In several cases, this ultimately led (in large part) to their later downfall. As economic cycles ebbed and and there was an inevitable drop in business, they lacked experienced teams with deep "bench strength" around them to help lead the company out of danger—in part, because they hadn't developed those individuals, such as through stretch assignments. Unfortunately, it often took the protegees' departures – and the arrival of outside leadership--to reverse course and right the ship.

AN EMPATHETIC APPROACH

Empathetic leaders see mentoring as one of the key functions of leadership and they have the confidence and foresight to mentor not only one-on-one, but also indirectly, by exposing their charges to other people, resources, and experiences that can help them. They understand that high-potential future leaders are eager for mentoring whenever and wherever they can find it, and they actively propel their protégés into situations where they will get the mentoring and add to their toolkits the knowledge and experiences they will need to succeed in future roles and organizations.

TIP #42:
MENTOR GLADLY AND WITHOUT RESERVATION

"A mentor is someone who sees more talent and ability within you than you see in yourself and helps bring it out of you."
Bob Proctor, coach and motivational speaker

"What you want in a mentor is someone who truly cares for you and who will look after your interests and not just their own. When you do come across the right person to mentor you, start by showing them that the time they spend with you is worthwhile."
Vivek Wadhwa, tech entrepreneur and academic

"Sometimes you have to let a person go so they can grow. Because, over the course of their lives, it is not what you do for them, but what you have taught them to do for themselves, that will make them a successful human being."
Marc Chernoff, author, personal development coach

"Getting the most out of life isn't about how much you keep for yourself, but how much you pour into others."
David Stoddard, songwriter

I once observed an exchange between coworkers that made me very sad and has stuck with me as a vital lesson in life and leadership all these many years. It was nothing shocking or scandalous – though it was heartbreaking in its own way: I saw someone repeatedly refuse their colleagues' requests to mentor them.

Reluctant Mentors
The reluctant mentor (aka, the Professor), was a towering figure in

our organization, and in the industry at large. Unfortunately, as much as he was a truly brilliant lecturer, he wasn't inclined to serve as a mentor, even though so many in the organization (and the industry) were very eager to learn from his wisdom in a close, ongoing relationship.

The scorned mentee – a charismatic and sensitive soul, himself a gifted teacher – was deeply deflated when his entrees were repeatedly rejected, dismissed, or ignored by the Professor, his professional idol. Several other team members experienced similar responses by the Professor, and all parties suffered from effects of the unfortunate missed opportunities over the years – with the rejected mentee wistfully wondering "what might have been," even to this day.

As disappointing as this circumstance was to observe, fortunately, my experience has been that most formal and informal leaders are eager and generous mentors. Empathetic leaders try hard to anticipate and understand the needs of others and try to address as many of these needs as feasible through coaching and mentoring. Below are several happy examples.

Mentoring with Gladness: Servant Leaders

Contrasted with the reluctant Professor above, I had the good fortune of observing how two senior operational leaders (George and Sy) approached mentoring and leadership. Hired to turn around a high-potential but undisciplined manufacturing facility, George and Sy both set about meeting the plant's employees where they were at (mentally, emotionally, and skill-wise), striving to take them to the next level and beyond.

When interacting with their new teams, they fielded (and solicited) all questions and actively sought out follow-up conversations with anyone on the team who exhibited special interest, enthusiasm, or eagerness to grow – including diamond-in-the-rough-type individuals who were untrained but champing at the bit to learn. They began to build up their young charges, both through one-on-one coaching, as well as by sending individuals and teams to external seminars, certification courses, and training sessions with experts in the field.

Unsurprisingly, as the facility began to take note of their efforts, morale quickly sky-rocketed and local engagement survey results went from below par to well above in a short period. This was due in large measure to a number of initiatives in which George and Sy's leadership and mentoring efforts played a prominent role.

Curmudgeon with A Heart of Gold

Coming into my first HR position out of college, I had virtually no knowledge of human resources—and even less of an idea as to what to expect as part of the professional world. It was working in this very large but quite-behind-the-HR-times organization that I met Henry.

Then in his mid-forties, Henry was a world-weary veteran of a Fortune 500 firm who had opted out of the corporate career ladder and found himself managing (sometimes much to his chagrin) the non-profit agency's pension matters. Correctly sensing right away that I had absolutely no clue what I had gotten myself into—and knowing that the head of the department was a kind but ineffectual leader who was unlikely to provide me with meaningful direction—Henry took me under his wing.

With great patience, he taught me the technical aspects of human resources, as well as how one works effectively in an organization (e.g., when to fight vigorously for a principle, or when to go with the flow and let nature take its course). Though he might occasionally growl at others, his kindness, support, and guidance at that crucial early stage in my career will never be forgotten.

Gentle Guidance from a Wise Behind-the-Scenes Figure

And then there was Sally, who walked into my professional life at the most opportune time for me. A veteran of the corporate wars as a longtime executive assistant (with two master's degrees), Sally was hired by the division president. Serving as part executive assistant and part behind-the-scenes "fixer," Sally calmly worked to support my boss, helping her grow her career at a critical juncture.

In her "spare" time, Sally went out of her way to lend support and guidance to this young-and-naive HR person in school-of-hard-knocks topics from efficient paper-processing to corporate politics, to say nothing of having quite a knack for knowing when a single male, living alone, could benefit from a home-cooked meal and supportive conversation with her and her equally kind and wise husband.

As one example, Sally saw me drowning in a sea of paperwork stacked on my desk (which we measured—sadly enough—in feet rather than inches!) She dedicated six weeks of her summer that year to getting me organized, teaching me the principle of "touch the paper once," and guiding me with great care through the sometimes-stormy waters of life in a rapidly-growing corporation. Though, after only two years of working together, I relocated to another division a thousand miles away, I still benefit almost every day of my working life from the insights Sally shared with me, even decades later.

AN EMPATHETIC APPROACH

It is tantalizing to have an expert in your midst who is unwilling to share their expertise with others who are eager for it. Empathetic leaders understand that they have members of their teams who are thirsty for knowledge to grow their skills and careers, and they eagerly give of their time to mentor these individuals, knowing that it will only increase the skill, morale, and performance of all involved.

CHAPTER 6
MANAGING YOUR CAREER

"Choose a job you love, and you will never have to work a day in your life."
Confucius, philosopher

"It's not what you achieve; it's what you overcome. That's what defines your career."
Carlton Fisk, Hall of Fame catcher

"Do not be too timid and squeamish about your actions. All life is an experiment."
Ralph Waldo Emerson, poet

Having worked our way through the prior chapters of hiring and building your teams, developing your culture, leading by example, and coaching and mentoring team members, we've finally arrived at the last step in the process of leading with empathy: addressing your own needs when managing your career.

While all of our reflections up to this point have encouraged leaders to be selfless and focused intently on the needs of *others*, there is nothing wrong with taking a few moments to consider and address *your own needs*, of course. By thoughtfully proceeding through your career, you are strengthening yourself so that you can be in position to help as many others as possible.

Tips and guidance in this final chapter include:

- Identifying when you have contributed all that you can for your current employer, and when you need (and deserve) a fresh breath in a new environment

- When you reach that point, knowing how to take your leave with graciousness and thoughtfulness for all concerned

- Identifying blind spots you may have regarding your current situation

- Knowing how to read the signs indicating that change is at hand, and having the courage to take the leap into the unknown

- Since we all have bosses, knowing how to communicate with your manager so that they hear the truths that you observe and owe it to them to share

- Finally, ways to recognize that you need a breather from your role, profession, organization, or industry, and how you can use time off to refresh and reenergize your feelings about your chosen career

• TIP #43:
DISCERN WHEN IT'S TIME TO MOVE ON

"Growth is painful. Change is painful. But nothing is as painful as staying stuck somewhere you don't belong."
Unknown

"If you're brave enough to say goodbye, life will reward you with another hello."
Paulo Coelho, author

"The secret of change is to focus all of your energy not on fighting the old, but on building the new."
Socrates, philosopher

The start of the new year is traditionally a time for fresh starts and career transitions. I was reminded of this one January not long ago when two close friends, both longtime, high-performing senior executives in their firms, confided their intentions to leave their positions as soon as they were able.

Both had similar reasons. In essence, they were misaligned with their company's values and culture and didn't have the heart to fight the battles any longer. When an empathetic leader finds themselves in similar circumstances, by focusing on what is fair for themselves (i.e., being empathetic to themselves), the go/no-go decision usually becomes fairly clear and easy to make.

Signs and Signals

When one—or certainly, a few—of the following are true, it may be time to move on to greener pastures:

- **Lack of resources** – If your division is consistently under-resourced and not given priority when capital expenses and operating budgets are decided on
- **Lack of trust** – If you've delivered strong financial results year after year, but ownership still doesn't trust you with profit-and-loss information for the division you are charged with managing
- **Lack of confidence** – If you no longer believe the organization will grow and develop into something more aligned with your vision for the future
- **Lack of strategy** – If you keep trying to discern a consistent strategy or direction based on executive decisions, but there's no clear pattern or perceptible way forward
- **Lack of shared values** – If, when push comes to shove, leadership regularly doesn't treat employees (or yourself) the way you would like
- **Lack of peer support** – If you're part of a leadership "team" where each member has their own very different agendas, none of which include supporting you or each other
- **Lack of hope** – If you no longer have the stamina to protect your team from the follies and foibles of management.

Why We Get Stuck

One might ask how intelligent, talented individuals, not lacking in career options, would put up with one, much less several, of the situations above for years before reaching the conclusion that it's time to move on. The truth, I believe, is that successful people are often positive-thinking and optimistic, confident in their ability to overcome obstacles, change the world or "fight city hall" and come out on the other side, to create better situations for all. This same spirit can blind us to the realities of our current environment.

Sometimes, we need to recognize that we've fought the good fight; we've done our best to improve the situation, but it has improved as much as it's going to improve, and it's time for us to move on – to sow seeds of hope and helpfulness in different and more fertile ground elsewhere.

AN EMPATHETIC APPROACH

How do you know for sure that it's time to move on? If you trust in the wisdom of your friends and counselors, you can confidently allow them to "take you off the hook." For example: When you confide your intentions to a trusted friend, and they smile kindly but knowingly and say, "So … what took you so long? I've been waiting to hear you say that for years!" Then, you know -- for sure.

Then, it's time to have empathy for *yourself.* Trust your friend's wisdom. And move on, with confidence – and clarity of mind and heart.

TIP #44:
KNOW HOW TO SAY GOODBYE

"Good night, good night! Parting is such sweet sorrow,
That I shall say good night till it be morrow."
William Shakespeare, Romeo and Juliet

"Great is the art of beginning, but greater is the art of ending."
Henry Wadsworth Longfellow, *poet*

In 2013, the announcement that Pope Benedict was resigning the papacy for health reasons stunned the world, as a papal resignation had not happened in six-hundred years. As this historic event unfolded, it offered several lessons in saying goodbye with dignity and purpose.

Key lessons that struck me included:

- **Some things don't need outside counsel**
  The fact that even Benedict's closest aides didn't have a hint of his pending resignation indicates the depth of conviction that he felt about his decision. "Unto thine own self be true," we're advised. In this case, the truth was clear to him, and he acted decisively, with clarity of purpose and peace of mind and heart. When clarity is present so strongly, no outside deliberations are necessary to provide cover or comfort— certainty of heart *is* the comfort.
- **It's not all about you**
  By canon (church) law, the pope has the right to preside over the church until his death. In his decision to resign, though, Benedict chose to place the needs of the many over his

personal ego or legacy concerns. In a statement, the pope observed that in order to govern "… both strength of mind and body are necessary, strength which in the last few months has deteriorated in me to the extent that I have had to recognize my incapacity to adequately fulfill the ministry entrusted to me." In doing so, he put the good of his organization—more than one billion souls globally, of a size and scope that requires vibrant daily leadership—ahead of himself.

- **Set up the next person for success**
  Benedict stepped down in the middle of the most important season in the church calendar (Lent). Few would have blamed him for hanging on a month longer, so that he might have the satisfaction of a "retirement tour," of sorts—i.e., leading one more season of Easter services before departing the world stage. With his choice of timing, though, Benedict guaranteed that his successor would be introduced to the world at the widely-watched Easter season services, thus launching the new pope forward to put his own stamp on his nascent papacy from the very first moment.

AN EMPATHETIC APPROACH

If the definition of empathy is considering the needs and feelings of others, I believe that Benedict clearly led with empathy in his decision to resign. We see in his actions the power that acts of humility can have on our organizations and ourselves. If we know our own hearts, and look to the needs of others, we will lead through service, for the greatest good.

TIP #45:
DECIDE WHEN TO TAKE THE FORKS IN THE ROAD

"When you come to a fork in the road, take it."
Yogi Berra, Baseball Hall of Famer, philosopher,
and American icon

"As you go through life, there are thousands of little forks in the road, and there are a few really big forks—those are moments of reckoning, moments of truth."
Lee Iacocca, CEO, Chrysler

"To be responsible, keep your promises to others.
To be successful, keep your promises to yourself."
Marie Forleo, entrepreneur, motivational speaker

Empathetic leadership is all about understanding the needs of others and then seeing how we can help them with our gifts, talents, and abilities. To that end, when the inevitable unexpected twists and turns in our lives and professional careers arise, as they surely do, empathetic leaders strive to understand the circumstances, assess available options, see where they can help best, and move forward.

In my own life and career, this has come up regularly. Here is one example for us to reflect on and learn from.

What We Want to Do Versus What Is Needed
Most professionals want to work on and lead projects that are strategic, exciting, and "leading edge." However, this might not always be what an organization truly needs. Sometimes (often), what is needed for success is old-fashioned nuts-and-bolts "blocking and

tackling"—not fancy strategies that may or may not work or be able to be executed well.

It takes a self-disciplined, well-grounded person (or team) to work on what is needed when it isn't necessarily what is "sexy" or likely to provide them immediate career growth, development, or visibility. There is always the (very valid) option to opt out and walk away to pursue other endeavors. If, for whatever reasons, you choose to stay, the question becomes how best to help where you are.

The Backstory

I spent several years working for a rapidly growing HR department in a division of a rapidly growing national firm. We were led by a talented HR exec with considerable vision, but unfortunately in this case, there was a blind spot in our collective vision as a team. While we were constantly focused on what we considered to be strategic initiatives, the organization was telling us that they needed something else, but we couldn't hear them.

They were saying, "Look, we need urgent help finding and hiring good people. Lots of them, and fast, for an extended period." The business was growing fast; the economy and the stock market were booming, and talented and qualified bodies were needed to fulfill orders and continue the growth trajectory. In the HR world, this is basic "blocking and tackling"—i.e., getting the company the people it needed to grow.

Unfortunately, somehow, we (HR) became enthralled only with strategic initiatives (i.e., new, leading edge, high-visibility projects) and the more mundane function of recruiting was relegated to after-thought status. Despite the business' well-communicated needs, recruiting didn't receive nearly as much time and attention as we should have given it. It certainly wasn't treated with an "all hands on deck, pedal to the metal" approach to getting requisitions filled that operations management (rightly) felt it deserved.

Our First Blind Spot: Ignoring Requests for (Recruiting) Help

As dozens, and then hundreds of openings piled up, we just weren't hearing or seeing what the organization really needed to help it move forward. In retrospect, of course, what possibly could have been more strategic than bringing in the talent that the organization needed and craved to fuel its growth? What could have been more worthy of a call to arms across our then 80-person HR team to urgently help fill every last position needed?

Alas, the call was never made. To say that we took our eye off the ball and completely missed the (repeated) messages that management was sending us would be an understatement.

Our Second Blind Spot: The Reorganization That We Missed

While, even all these years later, I cringe at the thought that we completely missed the red flags that the organization was putting up around recruiting, I'm even more aghast that we missed the second warning siren: when the company re-organized and we didn't notice. (Really.)

In short, we supported a division comprised of ten business units loosely tied together under a division president. We had been formed as an HR team several years earlier to help build and unify the culture, operations, and policies of the division. That effort was moving along, when … they disbanded the division. The division president moved on to a different role, and the business units split up with each reporting into different areas of the company. No one's job was really impacted except for the dozen of us on the division HR team, seeing as we no longer had a division to unify, which had been our *raison d'être*.

Somewhat remarkably, we spent the year after the reorganization was announced operating as if nothing had changed—i.e., still working to unify the division. Except that the division didn't exist anymore, and the business units (understandably) didn't want to be tied into something that didn't exist. Not surprisingly, shortly thereafter, they sat us down and explained (as a team) that "we could go now." Ouch. But they were right, of course.

What We Could Have Done

Once the division was disbanded, was there anything else we could have done to remain viable in the organization? In retrospect, there was.

The division HR team was comprised of talented, hard-working, people who had a great depth and breadth of skills and experience and could help lead any number of initiatives and projects. This was exactly the type of group that would have made excellent internal consultants. The only difference would have been that – as internal consultants -- instead of working on the projects *we* thought the organization needed (as we had done up until that point), we would have focused on what the *organization* wanted to do, and then helped them do it.

Unfortunately, *we completely missed it.* We were so tied up in our prior vision for HR, we didn't see that the world had changed and that we had the opportunity to still do good work, but in a different way. We came to a fork in the road ... and we didn't take it (primarily, because we didn't recognize it).

<u>AN EMPATHETIC APPROACH</u>

Our mistake in both cases—ignoring the company's obvious recruiting needs, and then not comprehending the opportunities that the reorganization offered us—occurred because we were focused only on *our* ideas and needs, and not on those of the people that we supported.

An empathetic leader will always keep their eyes and ears (and most importantly, their minds) open to the world of possibilities when the world changes and unexpected twists and turns come down the pike. Many great and unexpected opportunities may arise, as long as we have the humility and wisdom to see them – by seeing the needs of others.

TIP #46:
MANAGE UP: TELL YOUR BOSS
GENTLE TRUTHS

*"Just because an animal is large, it doesn't mean he doesn't want kindness;
however big Tigger seems to be, remember that he wants as much kindness
as young Roo."*
Pooh's Little Instruction Book

*"Good leadership requires you to surround yourself with people of diverse
perspectives who can disagree with you without fear of retaliation."*
Doris Kearns Goodwin, historian, author (A Team of Rivals)

"Truth never damages a cause that is just."
Mahatma Gandhi, Indian political and spiritual leader

One time, as I was helping a manager write a job description, he
leaned over and said, "There's one more requirement we need to
add." Waiting a beat, he smiled and then added, "The ability to make
the boss look good." We both laughed, but we both recognized the
truth in what he had said, too.

Politics or Empathy?

While the above statement may sound blatantly political, when seen
through the lens of empathy, it takes on a different tone. The
empathetic leader understands that "bosses are people, too," with the
same wants, needs, concerns, and insecurities as the rest of us, just at
a higher title or pay grade.

A wise longtime executive assistant once explained to me, "You have
to remember that bosses want a safe place to go at three o'clock, to

188

kick off their shoes, let go of their worries for a moment, and have their milk and cookies, just like everyone else." So true.

Rules of the Road

The question becomes, then, how we can we "manage up" and help our bosses look good, with integrity, serving the best interests of both our organization and our bosses? Four "rules" come to mind.

NOTE: The following examples concern competent, high-performing, well-meaning bosses. Incompetent, mean, or spiteful bosses are another case entirely, which is a story for another day.

- **Rule #1: Invite them into situations that play to their strengths --** I once supported a division president, Langdon, who was surprisingly quiet and shy in one-to-one or small group settings. (He was so modest and unassuming that, when my parents were first introduced to him, they thought he was the IT assistant). With a large crowd, though, he was a very passionate and engaging speaker. Therefore, when we invited him to kick off a "Welcome to the company" presentation on the day of an acquisition, we were quite surprised when he struggled mightily in telling the company's story to the crowd, as telling an impassioned tale of the division's history, goals and objectives was usually right in his sweet spot as a speaker.

  We later realized our mistake: we had given Langdon about twenty Power Point slides to speak from and he had been hamstrung by so many slides. The next time, we gave him only three or four items on an index card—no slides—and he was a hit! It turned out that, strapped down to a rigid script, he was wooden and unengaging. His casual, captivating personality only came out when he was free to make unscripted remarks, i.e., speaking from the heart. Once we figured this out, we kept inviting him to ad hoc speaking situations, and he shone.

- **Rule #2: Tell them gentle truths** -- For several years, I worked for a very selfless and patient boss who would always "take one for the team" and constantly subjugated his needs for the greater good of the organization. This is a wonderful quality … except when it's not (when it is taken to extremes). We all have strengths that, when overused or misapplied can be weaknesses (i.e., if one is "decisive," that's a good thing— but put "too" in front of "decisive" and it can become a negative, as in reactive, unyielding, inflexible, controlling, etc.) In my boss' case, his patience and selflessness led him to continually defer resources such as, staff, equipment, and funding that could have helped his division (and thus the organization) grow revenue because "the other department needed it more."

  Now, speaking truth to power is always a dicey proposition, so I'd probably suggest that "gentle truths" need to be told only about important matters. If the boss thinks he's a great golfer and he's not, that doesn't need to be shared. If, however, by being "too" something (too selfless, too decisive, etc.) in an instance or as a pattern of behavior, he's inadvertently hurting those he is trying to serve and protect, then he needs to be told. He may or may not agree or change his behavior, but he deserves to hear the other side of the story, to know how his actions are affecting the organization.

- **Rule #3: Help them be more self-aware** – As with most of us, executives sometimes have a difficult time recognizing quirks in themselves that others easily see. Examples include:
  - *The "Bounce-Back" Boss* -- who has the remarkable ability to bounce back from major setbacks literally

overnight, may need to be reminded that not everyone has this same capacity and that it is understandable for her chief lieutenant to take a day off to get his feet back on the ground after his mother's sudden diagnosis with a life-threatening illness

- *The "Gentle Giant" boss* -- The gentle-hearted but tall, physically imposing, and intense boss, who is always passionate when speaking about what needs to be done or improved in the organization, may need to be reminded that when someone of his size and bearing speaks intently while standing over someone of smaller stature, it can come across as intimidating or even threatening, regardless of his intention to the contrary

- *The "Not-As-Self-Aware-As-They-Think-They-Are" Boss* – It is very difficult to speak truth to a boss who is blind to their own problematic behaviors (such as speaking negatively about their executive peers to subordinates in public) that damage their credibility and are known to all – except themselves. When they can be spoken, though, your brave and empathetic candor may be doing them the biggest favor of their professional lives, helping them stop self-sabotaging their careers.

- **Rule #4: Help them hear the "voice of the people"** -- By definition, your boss is one level further removed from "the people" of the organization than you are, wherever you may stand in the hierarchy. If we trust that the wisdom of the organization is on the "shop floor" more than it is in the executive suite, we need to help the boss hear the voice of the shop floor, call center, etc. So, while they may not be inclined to stop and chat with the guys on the loading dock, so to speak, they may need to be reminded that doing so is vital to keeping their finger on the pulse of the organization.

Sounds of Silence

Sometimes, despite your best efforts, your truths aren't heard, whether delivered gently or with force. Yet, try we must.

Long ago, I supported an executive who devoted an extraordinary amount of their time to what was then called "employee communications" (what we would now probably call "messaging"). They labored over every email, blurb, and remark, concerned about presenting the intended message every time. The problem was, they labored over the messages so mightily, they never actually got sent (due largely to "paralysis by analysis").

When I pointed out that I felt the people needed to hear their voice, they were quite taken back, replying, "I feel like I spend all my time communicating." I had to explain that, while I was sure this was true in their mind, unfortunately, the team was hearing only silence, and they were getting more and more disconcerted, fearing that no news really meant the worst news, and were always expecting the other shoe to drop and the operation to close (which wasn't the case and didn't happen).

AN EMPATHETIC APPROACH

An empathetic leader is always concerned with understanding and addressing the needs of others (employees, vendors, customers, etc.). Having empathy for our leaders, we need to understand that they have the same blind spots and weaknesses as everyone else, and they need our support, understanding, and candor, just as we need theirs.

Sharing information and "gentle truths" may not change the boss' mind or alter their decision, but they need to be provided with the best information and counsel we can muster, so that they can make an informed judgement taking account of all facts and factors. Even if they don't want to hear your advice at that moment, a true leader will thank you for your candor—enhancing your credibility with the leader and your value to the organization.

TIP #47:
TAKE TIME FOR A PROFESSIONAL PILGRIMAGE

"The best way to find yourself is to lose yourself in the service of others."
— *Mahatma Gandhi, Indian political and spiritual leader*

"The real voyage of discovery consists not in seeking new landscapes, but in having new eyes."
Marcel Proust, French author

"The seeker embarks on a journey to find what he wants and discovers, along the way, what he needs."
Wally Lamb, The Hour I First Believed

"A journey of a thousand miles begins with a single step."
Lao Tzu, philosopher

I was very fortunate to embark on a long-desired personal pilgrimage during a recent summer vacation. This experience led me to wonder how many *professional* pilgrimages we hold in our hearts but never act on, and what our careers (and lives) would be like if we did. Out of empathy for themselves, I believe that we need to discern when we need a breather -- and then we must work toward providing it for ourselves.

A Journey, not a Destination
An informal definition of a pilgrimage is a quest or a journey of discovery and renewal. My personal pilgrimage was to the Shrine of Our Lady at Lourdes, France, a place of great healing and peace. Being there, even for just a few days, gave me insights and a sense of

194

life that I couldn't have gained if I hadn't planned, undertaken, and experienced the journey for myself.

Broadening our view from the spiritual to the professional, is there a vocational journey of discovery that you desire if only you had the time, money, freedom, etc.? Is there a new field that you've wanted to explore? Perhaps:

- You're a specialist in a nice area of your field who wants to become a generalist (or a manager), or vice versa
- You've been in a technical field for a long time, and you long to explore the creative arts (or vice versa)
- You've done what you've done for a long time. You know you're good at it, and you want to keep doing it ... but you'd dearly love to rediscover the passion you once had for it by stepping away for a while so that you can see things in a new light.

The Journey Begins with One Step

If you identify with any of the above, you may be perfectly poised for a pilgrimage. What's the catch? Starting, of course.

Taking the first step is the key. Doing the research ... making a plan ... then talking with your boss. Finding the expert or mentor you want to speak with or the course you want to take ... then sending your request or application. Sharing your ideas with your family, friends, or colleagues ... and then booking the trip.

What if it doesn't work out on your first try? What if you're turned down? What if you can't get approval? No worries. You win both ways:

- If everything falls into place, you get to embark on the journey. Imagine what it would feel like to have a new fresh breath about your career, and renewed passion for who you're helping and what you're learning and accomplishing!

- Or, if obstacles can't be overcome this time, taking that first step and getting stymied will give you even more resolve to make it work the next time you try. Either way, you've taken the first step of the journey. You're on the path of discovery and renewal. There's no stopping you now!

A Personal Reflection

Earlier in my career, I remember feeling "burnt out" after spending several intensive years managing the HR side of our company's many mergers and acquisitions. Even after building a small team to assist in this, and enjoying coaching and mentoring them to the fullest, it felt as if I needed a new fresh breath. The work got done, but not with the same enthusiasm and passion with which I had approached it in earlier days.

I approached my boss and proposed switching into other functions within the department. We had had a great relationship, and she always had been very supportive of me taking on new endeavors in the past, so I recall being quite taken back and bewildered when she was not at all sympathetic to my needs and was uninterested in pursuing different options in any way.

At the time, I didn't feel I could consider leaving that boss, that team, and that company after all that we had built together in the space of a few years. But from the vantage point of a few decades later, I wonder why not, and how things might have played out differently if I had.

Ironically, less than two years later, a re-organization led to a layoff that eventually freed me up to pursue other paths—just not quite in the way I had envisioned.

AN EMPATHETIC APPROACH

They say that charity begins at home and that we need to take care of and become strong ourselves before we can take care of and be strong for others. While the majority of this book argues for leadership through service to others first, in this one case I would propose that "unto thine own self be true" takes precedence. An emotionally mature, self-aware leader needs to recognize when their tank is dry and needs replenishing, and they must do so -- whether through a pilgrimage, sabbatical, taking on new assignments, or charting a new path in some way.

While it is important to have the self-discipline to delay gratifying your own needs, it is not healthy or feasible to ignore or discount your needs indefinitely. Find a way to give yourself that new fresh breath that you need, and everyone around you (family, friends, colleagues, teammates, etc.) will benefit as well from your renewed energy, excitement, and *joie de vivre*.

FINAL THOUGHTS

As these reflections draw to a close, I'd like to thank you for joining me in exploring the path of empathetic leadership through the prior forty-seven tips, in really what has been a career-long journey for me. I hope that the reading these thoughts on that journey has been beneficial for you; sharing them with you in this way has been a joy for me.

As a quick recap, we have found that empathetic leadership is all about identifying, understanding, and addressing needs of others so that we might help them use their talents and fulfill their professional destinies to the fullest, just as this enables us to do the same. This holds true throughout all steps along the leadership life cycle, from hiring and managing your team, to building your culture, coaching others, and leading by example while actively managing your career.

Along the way, we have observed the joys of mentoring gladly, of taking unleashing potential, building confidence, repairing relationships, solving the right problems, reversing downward spirals, lighting the way, acting with clarity, preparing the ground for success, and—to bring us full circle— mentoring without saying a word. In all these actions, by remaining humble, exuding gladness, and striving to improve the lives of all members of our teams, we will be doing all we can to make the world a better place and leave our mark with kindness, authenticity, and caring.

Post Script: A Capstone Experience

As I was preparing the final edits of this manuscript, I had the happy occasion to meet former colleagues for some festive, pre-holiday "reunion" lunches in favorite old spots. Everyone was in high spirits, renewing acquaintances and fondly sharing "war stories" from the "old days" together.

Amidst the reminiscing, I was struck by how powerful an impression past leaders had made on all of us, for both good and ill. Experiences with sincere, well-meaning leaders were recalled fondly and felt deeply, even as details of the events themselves faded into memory. The converse was equally and strikingly true: experiences with those seen as uncaring, distrusting, or arrogant leaders had left lingering, painful mental scars, even many years later.

This contrast served as a poignant reminder to me of the life-altering impact that empathetic leaders can have on individuals and organizations. To that end – with glasses raised, we toast all the good and light and hope and purpose that leading with empathy can bring, to so many. Cheers, good wishes, and encouragement to empathetic leaders everywhere!

Continuing the Conversation

I'm truly gratified by your interest in this topic as a leader, and I deeply appreciate you taking the time to ponder the reflections and observations I have put forth in this book. Should time ever permit you to share your impressions, I would love to hear your thoughts on the merits and practical implications of leading with empathy in your organization, team, and life. I look forward to continuing the conversation.

Michael Brisciana
michaelbrisciana@gmail.com

APPENDIX
SELECTED BIBLIOGRAPHY

As an additional resource, I wanted to share a selected listing of the books that have influenced my thinking about leading with empathy.

Bernardin, Joseph. *The Gift of Peace: Personal Reflections.* Chicago: Loyola Press, 1997.

Blanchard, Ken, and Garry Ridge. *Helping People Win at Work: A Business Philosophy Called "Don't Mark My Paper, Help Me Get an A" (Leading at a Higher Level).* Upper Saddle River, NJ: Pearson Prentice Hall, 2009.

Blanchard, Ken, and Spencer Johnson. *The New One Minute Manager.* New York: William Morrow, 2015.

Blanchard, Ken, and Margret McBride. *The 4th Secret of the One Minute Manager.* New York: William Morrow, 2008.

Bossidy, Larry, and Ram Charan. *Execution: The Discipline of Getting Things Done.* New York City: Crown Business, 2009.

Browne, Steve. *HR on Purpose: Developing Deliberate People Passion. Alexandria, VA:* Society For Human Resources Management. 2017.

Buscaglia, Leo F. *Living, Loving, and Learning.* New York: Holt, Rinehart and Winston, 1982.

Cain, Susan. *Quiet: The Power of Introverts in a World That Can't Stop Talking.* New York: Broadway Books, 2013.

Carreyrou, John. *Bad Blood: Secrets and Lies in a Silicon Valley Startup*. New York: Knopf, 2018.

Collins, Jim. *Good to Great: Why Some Companies Make the Leap and Others Don't*. New York: HarperBusiness, 2001.

Covey, Stephen R., and Rebecca R. Merrill. *The Speed of Trust: The One Thing That Changes Everything*. New York: Free Press, 2008.

Dyer, Wayne D. *Excuses Be Gone: How to Change Lifelong, Self-Defeating Thinking Habits*. New York: Hay House Inc., 2011.

Fulghum, Robert. *All I Really Need to Know I Learned in Kindergarten: Uncommon Thoughts on Common Things*. New York: Ballantine, 2004.

Goodwin, Dorins K. *No Ordinary Time: Franklin and Eleanor Roosevelt: The Home Front in World*. New York: Simon & Schuster, 1995.

Grote, Dick. *Discipline Without Punishment: The Proven Strategy That Turns Problem Employees into Superior Performers*. New York: Amacom, 1995.

Hsieh, Tony. *Delivering Happiness: A Path to Profits, Passion, and Purpose*. Grand Central Publishing: New York, 2013.

Hunter, James C. *The Servant: A Simple Story About the True Essence of Leadership*. Roseville, CA: Prima, 1998.

Isaacson, Walter. *Einstein: His Life and Universe*. New York: Simon & Schuster, 2008.

Kerpen, Dave. *The Art of People: 11 Simple People Skills That Will Get You Everything You Want*. New York: Crown Business, 2016.

Krznaric, Roman. *Six Habits of Highly Empathic People*. Greater Good Magazine, University of California – Berkeley, November 27, 2012

Lafair, Sylvia. *Don't Bring It to Work: Breaking the Family Patterns That Limit*

Success. San Francisco: Josey-Bass, 2009.

Merton, Thomas. *The Seven Storey Mountain*. Boston: Mariner Books, 1999.

Milne, AA. *Winnie the Pooh*. London: Methuen Publishing, 1926.

Scott, Susan. *Fierce Conversations: Achieving Success at Work and in Life One Conversation at a Time*. New York: Berkley, 2004.

Sinek, Simon. *Why Leaders Make Their People Feel Safe*. TED Talks. www.youtube.com, 2014.

Waterman, Jr, Robert H., and Thomas J. Peters. *In Search of Excellence: Lessons from America's Best-Run Companies*. New York: HarperBusiness, 2006.

Welch, Jack, and John A. Byrne. *Jack: Straight from the Gut*. New York: Grand Central Publishing, 2003.

ABOUT THE AUTHOR

Michael Brisciana is a Human Resources executive with a passion for servant leadership. He strives to help organizations, teams, and individuals achieve their fullest potential by aligning hearts, minds, skills, and passions with business needs for greatest mutual benefit.

He has served in HR leadership roles with Fortune 500 organizations, educational consulting firms, global manufacturing and distribution companies, and non-profit organizations across a more than twenty-five-year professional career.

Michael holds an MBA from Loyola University Chicago and a B.S. in Business Administration from Bucknell University, along with senior HR certifications from SHRM and HRCI. He has previously published two HR management guidebooks.

Michael is always eager to share ideas about leadership and corporate culture. He can be reached at michaelbrisciana@gmail.com , on LinkedIn at https://www.linkedin.com/in/michael-brisciana , and on Twitter: @MBrisciana_HR .

LIT

Made in the USA
Middletown, DE
13 January 2023

22093369R00128